Pen-ultimates

To Philomena

Acknowledgments

We wish to thank The Christian Century Foundation for permission to reprint material which appeared first on the pages of *The Christian Century*, from 1960 to early 1963. We also thank Rita of Cascia, patroness of desperate causes.

M.E.M. and D.G.P.

A Private Word
With The Reader

Should any particular column or chapter offend you for any reason, please communicate with the author of that chapter. You can contact him at this address:

> Mr. Dean Peerman
> 407 South Dearborn Street
> Chicago, Illinois

> MARTIN E. MARTY

A Private Word
With The Reader

Should any particular column or chapter offend you for any reason, please communicate with the author of that chapter. You can contact him at this address:

> Mr. Martin E. Marty
> 407 South Dearborn Street
> Chicago, Illinois

> DEAN G. PEERMAN

Contents

Contents

Pen-ultimates

Introduction

The Penultimate Aspect

Simeon Stylites the First, as you will learn on the ultimate pages of this book, died in 459. A pillar saint, he looked down in scorn on the world around him. Simeon Stylites the Second, who died in 1960, was a saint without a pillar, and unlike his predecessor looked with loving amusement on his world. The second Simeon sometimes owned up to the name Halford E. Luccock, taught at Yale University, and wrote a weekly column on the second-last page of *The Christian Century* magazine. It had the distinction of being the best-known, best-loved, most quoted, most plagiarized, most plundered column in religious journalism. Simeon stood in a long line of personalities in the pseudonymous columns of the magazine. Before him were Safed the Sage, Quintus Quiz, and others.

Just what Simeon has been doing since his translation to the pillared halls above, we of course cannot ascertain. But he certainly has done nothing to turn up successors to himself among the mortals. Imitators, yes, but no successors. Is it a disturbing sign of the times that instead of being occupied by a charismatic columnist, a beloved personality, his column is now taken up by an Organization, by the group mind? Not that the two authors of this book constitute a group, though they depend on the magazine's whole staff and a large segment of its readership for help. But for the first time in its history the column is unsigned by nym or pseudonym. Instead, it is anonymously devoted to an idea, or better, an aspect—a way of looking at life.

Needless to say, the authors are not pre-empting title to succession in the line of Simeon Stylites. They are to be conceived of as custodians, temporary time-biders in filling the space.

1

More or less, though on a different scale, like Pope John. But just as the pontiff relished the job and ran away with it, so did the authors decide to make the enjoyable most out of the task assigned to them. On these pages are distilled some of their efforts.

After Simeon's death there was a column to fill. Nature abhors a vacuum. So do editors. Advertisers in the *Century* liked the second-last page—the "Pen-ultimate" page—and vied for position on it. Readers expected some lightening of the pace before they turned the last page of the magazine. From time to time, imitators of Simeon sent in contributions; some of them were worthy of publication and appeared over the authors' signatures in the column. But no one yet has emerged who has Simeon's stamina; he could outlast the best of them. By default the column fell to the editorial staff. Simeon's technique was gently syncopated counterpoint: he would take an offbeat cultural theme and set it against an offbeat religious tempo. Ours is a different technique: looking at things and juxtaposing them. (Thus at least it is not imitation. The pillar is still vacant.)

The editorial staff had long felt the need for a catchall column. The editorial pages were desacralized once in a while with a miscellany corner colloquially called "Grab Bag." But the fore part of the magazine offered limited opportunities for unstaid comment; the decor and the decorum in the primary regions are too decorous. Some of the contagion and comment that saw the light of day only on the office bulletin board, or received a hearing at the *Century* staff's coffee hour, deserved a larger public and found its place just inside the back cover. You might say it *just* barely made it into the magazine. To our satisfaction, the new column began to pick up readers and, we soon learned, some sympathizers and admirers (we have framed both their letters to the editor). It began to attract contributors who were willing to permit ruthless plagiarism—the root "teleological suspension of the ethical" for all columnists—for the sake of the cause.

The column also did not lack critics. They tended to appear whenever one particular note was struck. Any ironic reference to religious affairs, any parodying of ceremonies and prayers seemed to offend a few. Perhaps these critics are correct in their attitude; perhaps the unholy parodies of the holy do not themselves deserve parody. This is not the place to argue the point. But it does provide the occasion to detail how we conceive penultimacy and its intentions. (It is also the place to thank Harold E. Fey and Kyle Haselden, editors of the *Century,* for permitting us to go on even after several people wrote "Please Cancel Immediately Unless You Get Rid of . . ." letters.)

But to get back to penultimacy. We have titled this introductory essay "The Penultimate Aspect." We do so deliberately. We could have said *stance,* or *attitude,* or *posture,* but those words are very much in vogue and we wanted something new; you cannot sell books without some new theological nuance being brought to bear! It is important to remember that in choosing words you must be careful not to let them mean exactly what the first dictionary definition says. So we settled on "aspect," which does not exactly mean "a way of looking at things" in the first dictionary definition.

To the point of "penultimate." The column was, we like to think, named accidentally. Our fellow Associate Editor, Miss Margaret Frakes, one sacred hour of coffee suggested the name "Pen-ultimate" for the column. Why? The column was generally the last thing the staff penned each week before the deadline. It appeared on the penultimate page of the journal. (Just about that time another magazine, we later learned, was sending around second-last notices bearing the word PENULTIMATE in large letters. Had we known that, we still would have named our column "Pen-ultimate." As we've noted, we are plagiarists at heart.)

To get back to that coffee hour. Miss Frakes's suggestion nearly made the two undersigned hitherto pseudonymous personages spill their coffee. Her practical definition was just loaded with theological finesse. "Penultimate" had been used by the great German thinker Dietrich Bonhoeffer (in his

Ethics) to describe a very important category. In providing a name, Miss Frakes cued us to the aspect we wished to assume. Since this book contains approximately 30,000 words and since she provided the first and most important of them, we herewith promise her .0003 per cent of the royalties.

One of our college professors gave us a rule of life that well describes the penultimate aspect. He told us that there were things in life which one must take very, very, very seriously—but not too seriously. When we defined penultimacy in that spirit, one wounded reader wrote in to say he had detected a Bonhoefferian category, and expressed disappointment that the detection pointed only to a coincidence. Actually, we had had Bonhoeffer in mind when we baptized the column. But we were then, and still are, diffident about associating Bonhoeffer's distinction of terms with our (necessarily) abrupt dealing with the category in weekly comment on religious affairs.

For Bonhoeffer, the term "penultimate" related to the Second Article of the Christian faith. The "ultimate thing" was God's act of justifying man. But, wrote the theologian, the Christian must also guard the "things before the last," the penultimate things. The penultimate is that which is hidden and which remains, even though the ultimate entirely annuls and invalidates it. The penultimate is everything which precedes the justification of the sinner: hunger, injustice, loneliness, disorder, "conditions of the heart, of life, and of the world which impede the reception of grace in a special way, namely, by rendering faith infinitely difficult" (*Ethics*, p. 94).

In dragging the concept of penultimacy from those sacred precincts into the common hall of journalism we have tried carefully to give it new definition. In our use, it has to do with the human potentials and the human obstructions with the second-last things that must be taken very seriously, but not too seriously; that must be appraised or reckoned with or disposed of so that the ultimate can be seen in freedom.

Most of the penultimacy reckoned with in this book is related to the folk religions of America which parallel the Christian faith. Here we celebrate their rituals, examine their institutions, review their liturgies, relish their ethos—and look at them in a different light. Along the way, therefore, the column picks up a distinct attitude, or aspect, which perhaps can best be defined by what it is not.

Unlike most of the humor in Protestant (and other) religious journals, that of penultimacy is not cute. For some reason or other, some editors—and with them, we must assume, most church people—take their relief from the Holy by recourse to sweet cartoons about Sunday school, snappy sermon starters, and priest-rabbi-minister "cute" jokes. For another thing, the columns are not, and are not intended to be, funny. It would be intolerable to have to think of putting together something that people would laugh at every week. There is not a joke in the whole book. Nor does the genre, even though it occasionally issues in parody, represent sarcasm. Generally it is too self-directed to be characterized that way. And most consistently, the penultimate aspect lets things speak for themselves. For the most part we place them into context or try to bring out hidden aspects by juxtaposing them against other things equally in need of context.

We are tempted to say that penultimacy relates to Søren Kierkegaard's category "humor." You may recall that the Danish sage placed humor as the penultimate category among the three spheres of existence (the aesthetic, the ethical, the religious). Two boundary zones correspond to these; humor separates the ethical from the religious. We felt that so elevated a category was just a notch too high, and tried "irony" instead— "irony" being the zone between the aesthetic and the ethical.

Writes Kierkegaard in his *Concluding Unscientific Postscript:* "Irony is a synthesis of ethical passion which infinitely accentuates inwardly the person of the individual in relation to the ethical requirement—and of culture, which infinitely abstracts externally from the personal ego, as one finitude among all the other finitudes and particularities. . . . Irony is an existential determination . . . a specific culture of the spirit" (pp. 449–50).

Well, we're glad we cleared that up. But irony does not quite cover the subject either. Particularly in our time, irony is an "incognito" device whose user remains too uninvolved—at least in an ethical sense. As we conceive penultimacy vis-à-vis *The Christian Century,* it enables the rest of the magazine to pursue its way on behalf of prophetic causes in which we wish very much to be counted and involved, causes which we hope to see prevail. Penultimacy keeps the pressure on; irony permits one to be "off the hook." Reliance on irony would contradict the intentions of the authors as Associate Editors of the *Century.*

Benjamin De Mott, in his study of "sick" comics in *Hells and Benefits,* offers intelligent comment on a form of irony with which penultimacy is not to be identified. In a section called "Varieties of Indifference," he scolds the sick comedians for using irony to deny and frustrate social hope. Their brand of irony assumes an inner world, which the informed inhabit, and an outside world of dolts (an attitude parodied in "One More 'In' and 'Out'" in Chapter 2 of this book). In this inner world, irony can be a paralyzing category: indifferent about causes, distinctionless, self-protective, hostile, intent on forming elites. And it can issue in a way of looking at life which cancels out *all* causes and leaves no sides, no valid issues. Penultimacy, however, is based on a great concern for "ultimate things" (see Chapter 4, "Positive Thinking"). Where things ultimate and holy are concerned, penultimacy leaves ample room for sermons, counsel, acts of love, editorialization, prophecy, creative silence.

A few of our columns touch on events-of-the-day which may no longer seem memorable. Such chronicling will, however, convey to the reader a sense of currency about the parareligious life of America in the early 1960's. But most of the columns are loosely clumped by category without chronological interest: press releases, amusements, liturgies and dramas, advertisements, notices, crusades—they are all here. For the important causes to whose path they would clear ground, we refer the curious to the other pages of *The Christian Century* magazine. For an explanation of that serious concern and how our love for penultimate matters relates to it, we return once more to the twice-removed inspiration for this category, Dietrich Bonhoeffer, who in his prison letter wrote:

"It is only when one knows the ineffability of the name of God that one can utter the name of Jesus Christ. It is only when one loves life and the world so much that without them everything would be gone, that one can believe in the resurrection and the new world. It is only when one submits to the law that one can speak of grace, and only when one sees the anger and wrath of God hanging like grim realities over the head of one's enemies that one can know something of what it means to love them and forgive them" (*Prisoner for God*, p. 79).

1 Press Releases

We Dreamed
a Press Release

**SPECIAL TO DENOMINATIONAL PERIODI-
CALS AND RELIGIOUS YOUTH MAGAZINES.
PHOTOGRAPHS AVAILABLE.**

The seventh annual Miss Hemisphere contest, held this year in the Virgin Islands, had its grand finale last night. This increasingly popular contest solves a problem for religious magazines: the Miss Universe and Miss America contests are staged more than a month apart, leaving a public-relations gap for religious monthlies and biweeklies; if it were not for the Miss Hemisphere contest many of these publications would, for one or two summer issues, have to do without photos of religious beauty-contest lovelies.

The genial Rev. "Jerry" Jurgens, church adviser to the girls aspiring to be queen of the hemisphere, declared: "The *koinonia* developed by these young ladies is revelant [*sic*] to the Protestant interpretation of life." Said chaperone Eileen Franciosa at a press conference: "Two decades ago churchmen criticized beauty contests for appealing to the lusts of the flesh. We are happy to say they now embrace the beauties, for the contests now accent talent."

Talent was abundant this year. The runner-up, a smiling, blue-eyed blonde Methodist, Sherry Varee (36-24-36) of Pittsburgh, played a Bach *chaconne* on the ocarina. Third place went to smiling, blue-eyed blonde Presbyterian Sandra Doll (36-24-36), Miss Michigan. Sandra's talent shone forth in her essay, "How I Would Bring Peace": she suggested a summit

9

conference bringing together Pope John, Nikita Khrushchev, Billy Graham, Albert Schweitzer, and Bert Parks. Fifth place went to Miss Minnesota, smiling, blue-eyed blonde Gina Gustafson (36-24-36), a Lutheran. Her enthusiasm for the contest was manifested in the way she spoke out against the show's critics: "Bathing beauty contests, nothing! These are talent and character shows. Miss Hemisphere of 1959 proved that; she became tap-dancer-in-residence at the Ogallala, Nebraska, television station." Congregationalist Laura Lane (36-24-36), a smiling, blue-eyed blonde Miss Maine, eighth place, was voted "Miss Talent of 1962"; however, a broken bathing-suit strap kept her from winning the Miss Hemisphere title. Miss Lane's remarkable versatility was displayed in a number in which she smilingly recited T. S. Eliot's "The Waste Land" while performing an interpretive dance. "We all have high aspirations," she panted afterward; "Miss Hemisphere of 1958 went on to many successes and has even appeared before the McClellan committee."

Seventh place went to a smiling, blue-eyed blonde Baptist, Mary Firbee (36-24-36), Miss Panama. Her prize was awarded for her answer to the question "What does hemispheric youth need?" Her impromptu answer: "I believe that high ideals are most important." Ninth place went to smiling, blue-eyed blonde Episcopalian Margaret Law (36-24-36), Miss Massachusetts, who in her talent act read portions of the Eichmann trial.

Cooed Miss Texas, smiling, blue-eyed blonde Karen Crane (42-24-36), a Southern Baptist: "I think it's so nice that the United States gets fifty representatives, one for each state, while all those foreigners from Latin America get only one per country." Miss Crane, who did not place in the talent events, announced that she is marrying an oil man next Tuesday.

Contest winner this year was smiling, brunette Maria Guadalupe Anunciacion (36-24-36), Miss Bolivia.

Please
Release Us!

Quoting publicity releases is not considered plagiarism. We've decided to quote a release about some releases—and right now we feel relieved that doing so will release us from attempting much in the way of original work for this week's Pen-ultimate. The document, which comes from the producers of the film *King of Kings,* is a boastful summary of thirty-two handouts concerning every aspect of their opus, and it lists the types of newspaper and magazine columns for which each release is designed. *Century* critic Tom F. Driver has already done justice to the content of the movie, which has been almost universally condemned by Protestants, Catholics, Jews, and agnostics for its dullness, its tastelessness, its willful distortions of the life of Jesus. We believe we can render a service to readers in indicating by quotation one of the reasons why we are suspicious of such films. Let's look at the titles of some of the releases the producers boast they have distributed: "Bringing Story of Jesus Christ to Screen Long-Time Dream of Producer Samuel Bronston"; "Director Nicholas Ray's Prime Purpose Was to Make Living Reality of the Story of Jesus"; "In Spain, a Rock Is a Rock!"; "The Man Who Plays Christ."

But now it begins to get interesting: "Glamor Is the Word for Rita Gam—a 530-word biographical story on the actress who portrays the beautiful but wicked Herodias in *King of Kings.* For drama pages."

"Salome Was a Teen-Ager—a 550-word story on Brigid Bazlen, aimed at teen-age moviegoers."

"Kings of Kings Director Disagreed with Leonardo da Vinci in Filming the Last Supper."

"How to Keep a Husband at Home and Alive—a 1,300-word story on Rita Gam, who says boredom is . . ."

"One of the Greatest Make-Up Tricks Is Not to Look Made-up. . . . For women's and beauty pages." [This is *King of Kings* yet!]

"Maid's Night Out. . . . For women's and cooking pages."

By now, faithful reader, surely you must want us to say something original. Always obliging, we herewith make a suggestion for an indoor sport for Christmas parties. Your guests are to assume that they have the publicity job for the coming Italian film of the *whole* Bible, the object of the game being to come up with ideas for releases and their appropriate columns. Some starts:

"Judas Outlines Silver-Polishing Scheme," a 500-word release on how the glint was kept on the betrayal silver, with advice to housewives who have the tarnish problem. For housewives, coin-collectors.

"Tamar Was a Teen-Ager." Just 1,800 words; for teen-agers and aging men.

"Jet-Age Elijah." A 900-word article on how the astronauts were consulted on technical details in launching the flaming chariot. For NASA and other government officials, jet pilots, all people named Elijah, and the National Safety Council.

"Saul Was a Seven-Footer." A sparse 900 words on why Wilt Chamberlain was elected to play the part of the tall man of the tribe of Benjamin. For sports columns.

"How I Was Cheated Out of a Part." Approximately 1,100 words on how Gina Lugubriosa was removed from the film after it was learned that her role, that of Susanna, was really apocryphal.

The canonical field is yours.

Babel
Babble

Jim Bishop or somebody like him is always telling us exactly what happened where in the ancient biblical world. Such information inspires sundry expeditions to Ararat to find the Ark, or to the Dead Sea to find Sodom (ancient version). Now

Authenticated News, New York City—credit line is requested—
has sent us a picture of the Tower of Babel by Gustave Doré,
and a release by one Jacques Vaneau: "Twenty-five Centuries
After Its Destruction, the Tower of Babel Is Being Rebuilt."
You can write Authenticated if you wish to authenticate
(people do not always believe what Pen-ultimates say). Is the
release a hoax? Was it concocted by someone out of touch with
reality? Is it for real? When you write a column such as this
you *have* to believe that such things are for real. Now Un-
authenticated News Bureau (*don't* write to it) has come
through with a confirmation—to wit, this memo:

FROM: Ecumenical Archaeo-Architectural Service, Office of the
Assistant Executive Secretary in Charge of Expediting Inter-
denominational Co-ordinators.
To: Interdenominational Co-ordinators.
RE: Rebuilding Tower of Babel on old foundations.

1. Translations of this memo are available.

2. Stress the fact that we must work fast. The Orthodox Archbishop of Babylon and the Catholic Bishop of Birs-Nimroud
have shown interest. The Tigris-Euphrates Independent Baptist
Association is trying to get ahead of us.

3. In response to fundamentalist pressure, Rudolf Bultmann
will be dropped from the building committee. He contends that
the foundations of old Babel are mythological. We say: If they
don't exist, we will have to invent them. Take a strong conservative stand; that is the prevailing mood.

4. Frank Lloyd ("Mile-High Skyscraper") Wright's death
deprives us of architectural counsel. He was theologically shaky:
he said, "God is on top." Shall we use Mies van der Rohe?
What about his theology? He said, "God is in the details."

5. Zoning is a problem. Threaten a boycott of Babel mer-
chants if they continue to resist religious use of multipurpose
structures.

6. For fund raising we have contacted the "Group Organization of United Giving Energies" (GOUGE) for a three-year
fund drive. It stresses Christian motivation: "Only one life

'twill soon be past, only what's done for Christ will last." Be sure to point out tax deductibility.

7. The ladies have got the kitchen out of hand; it is now bigger than the 183rd-floor chapel. To get it back in shape we have asked as consultants the Rev. Charles Shedd, author of *Pray Your Weight Away*, and Deborah Pierce, author of *I Prayed Myself Slim*.

8. Authenticated News says that "gold and gems are in the basement" of the old tower. Can we raffle these off or use them as door prizes at the Ecumenical Mardi Gras? We can get tax exemption. Don't use bingo—that's Catholic.

9. Material Service competition is keen. We cannot use laminated trusses—the lightning danger is great.

10. We are negotiating with Forest Lawn for cemetery rights next door, and with Berlitz, in case we again get interference from above at Babel.

2 Fun and Games

One More
"In" and "Out"

Before the "in" and "out" game is played for the last time, we would like to set forth a religious version. "In-ness," remember, does not necessarily imply "ought-ness"; what is "in" is not necessarily what should be "in," and vice versa. At any rate, our eyes, ears, and intuitions report the following:

In: baroque organs, Karl Barth at Gettysburg, the nineteenth century, the Hermeneutical Problem, chalices, saying you liked the movie better than the book, Robert McAfee Brown, Schleiermacher, SANE placards, post-Bultmannism, William Stringfellow, twenty-minute sermons, Natural Law, H. Richard Niebuhr, *The New Testament Octapla,* used or clinker bricks in church construction, the term "conversion," the theology of John Wesley, rocking chairs, John Fry of *Presbyterian Life,* mosaic-glass windows, John Cage, Ann Landers, Ted Sorenson, the Council of Chalcedon, *Mater et Magistra,* fraternal workers, Gerhard Ebeling, *Last Year at Marienbad,* Rembrandt, *motive,* Peter Berger, Marc Chagall, James Baldwin, Heinrich Schuetz, "Peanuts," John Ciardi, Federico Fellini, Edmund Wilson, Nobel prize winner Luthuli.

Out: cushioned pews, syncretism, the Albert Schweitzer cult, *King of Kings,* High Church, Pitirim Sorokin, Low Church, Malotte's "Lord's Prayer," flowers at funerals, rheostats on sanctuary lighting systems, quoting Robert Burns in sermons, Catherine Marshall and Anne Morrow Lindbergh, cute bulletin boards in front of churches, POAU, Cardinal Spellman, Nels Ferré's homemade adjectives like "agapaic," the prayer of St. Francis of Assisi, Herman Wouk, Harry Golden, Salvador

Dali, Sallmann's "Head of Christ," Volkswagens, clerical collars on the unordained, electronic organs, most sick jokes, van Gogh reproductions, Moral Re-Armament, dialogue sermons, Pleasantville, *Six Crises,* calling church buildings "plants," colored choir robes, background music for the liturgical use of the Lord's Prayer, Forest Lawn, money-raising gimmicks for churches, people who make "in" and "out" lists, bomb shelters, TV re-runs, Stanley Kramer, the Rat Pack, J. Howard Pew, *The Sound of Music.*

So Far In as to Be Almost Out: cell groups, Albert Camus, the New Quest, J. D. Salinger, Rouault, Zen, nondirective counseling, Taizé, Robert Frost, the *Village Voice,* Mies van der Rohe, Harry Bertoia, John Glenn.

So Far Out as to Be Almost In: the Akron plan, harmoniums, gospel hymns as folk songs, Albrecht Ritschl, the King James Version, Gothic architecture, taking "out" lists and using them as "in" lists, Jacqueline Kennedy, General de Gaulle, nostalgia over Jack Paar.

Sacred
Arithmetic

Should public funds be spent for parochial school textbooks? Obviously not for religious texts—but many Roman Catholics argue that such funds could, without violating the Constitution, be appropriated for books on secular subjects. "How can there be any religious doctrine in an algebraic formula?" the argument goes. Having completed extensive research on the matter for the National Council of Churches' department of religious liberty, George R. la Noue reports that "religious doctrine can be taught in an algebraic formula or, at least, in an arithmetic book." Mr. La Noue cites these examples from Catholic texts: (1) "The book about St. Theresa costs $2.00. The book about St. Joseph costs $1.05. Find the difference in the prices of the two books." (2) "It was Mother Mary's birthday. Ann brought three flowers and Jerome brought two flowers to put in front of Mother Mary's statue. How many flowers in all were put in front of the statue?"

At first we were appalled at such unimaginative, contrived, pedestrian pedagogy. But being appalled is too negative a reaction for us to nurture long, and we soon began envisioning all kinds of possibilities for sacred arithmetic in future Protestant texts. Try these samples of ours:

(1) Divide the amount you put in the collection plate last Sunday into the amount you tipped the waitress Saturday night.

(2) Reduce the number of subscribers to *America* magazine. Add to the number of subscribers to *The Christian Century, Concern,* and *Christianity and Crisis.*

(3) How far is it from Belmont, Massachusetts, to any place else via a candy truck? How far from Tulsa, Oklahoma, to any place else by circuit riding?

(4) What are the square roots of Paul Tillich's theology?

(5) What was Fred Schwarz's take-home pay in 1961? What will it be three years from now?

(6) Compare attendance at Billy Graham's Chicago Crusade (just getting under way) with attendance at (a) Chicago White Sox games during the same period; (b) Chicago Cubs games. What does this tell us about the National League?

(7) How far away is Karl Barth's Wholly Other? Multiply this times Kierkegaard's infinite qualitative distinction. Then relax.

(8) Our church cost $700,000; their church cost $400,000. Which one is better?

(9) Tickets to the First Baptist fish fry cost $1.50 each; 400 were sold. If a state tax were levied on this venture, how much would it be? How much would such taxation slow down the Kingdom of God if three fish fries were held each year?

(10) How often was the word "relevant" used in the last campus sermon you heard? Divide this by the number of times its use *was* relevant.

(11) If Norman Vincent Peale's *The Power of Positive Thinking* was on *The New York Times*'s best seller list X

number of weeks and his most recent book was *not* on that
list *Y* number of weeks, what does this tell us about *The New
York Times?*

(12) What is the average number of children in the Roman
Catholic families on your block? In Protestant families on your
block? Have you any suggestions?

Q.E.D.

Aungells
and Goosts

Is Christian faith born of obscurity, romanticism, archaism,
poetic fancy, ignorance? Is it threatened by clarity, commonplaceness, currency, prosaic factuality, awareness? To read certain literary critics (Bergen Evans and Brooks Atkinson writing
in *The New York Times,* and Norman Ross in the *Chicago
Daily News,* come to mind) one would think so. Almost invariably the *littérateurs* criticize new Bible translations, imply-
ing that all falls apart when the original *koine* ("common")
Greek is commonly translated. They have been especially hard
on the New English Bible. Ross sees the incarnation threatened
if the K.J.V.'s "great with child" becomes the N.E.B.'s "she
was pregnant." Evans, as an agnostic and a professor of
English, feels that his students who believe will cease to believe
if the romance of the K.J.V. is out. Atkinson declares that the
N.E.B., missing some of the mystery and terror of the sacred
myth, loses contact with Christian origins.

We would help these romanticizers, and we are greatly aided
by a new biblical tool: a masterful and majestic compilation of
eight English Bible versions on facing pages, *The New Testament Octapla,* edited by Luther A. Weigle. Why not put it to
work? Our thesis: If faith is enhanced by the K.J.V., why stop
at the halfway point? Why not have *more* obscurity, romanticism, archaism, poetic fancy, ignorance of biblical intentions?
We can help the literary critics by illustrating with a non-

crucial *Octapla* passage, chosen for reasons of reverence for cruciality. Picture Evans and Atkinson finding new faith via this progression (pardon, retrogression):

1. "Instantly an angel of the Lord struck [Herod] down, because he had usurped the honour due to God; he was eaten up with worms and died" (Acts 12:23, N.E.B.). "Eaten up" is too crude. No English student could believe at this point.

2. "And immediately the angel of the Lord smote him, because he gave not God the glory: and he was eaten of worms, and gave up the ghost." At this point the Evans-Atkinson club allows for the possibility of faith; this is K.J.V.

3. "And forthwith an Angel of our Lord strooke him, because he had not given the honour to God: and being consumed of wormes, he gave up the ghost" (Rheims, 1582). That "strooke" is a deft stroke. Maybe the critics will have to take faith seriously themselves, if we get still more obscure and remote!

4. "But immediately the Aungell of the Lorde smote him, because he gave not glorie unto God, he was eaten of wormes, and gave up the Gost" (Geneva, 1562). Careful; our friends find their hearts strangely warmed by that romantic "Aungell." "Gost" is another nuance opening the way to conversion.

5. "And immediately the angel of the Lorde smote him, because he gave not God the honoure, and he was eaten of wormes, and gave up the goost" (Tyndale, 1525). There, that's it! Why does Evans starve his students on King James; why does Atkinson not worry about *its* commonplaceness? This "gave up the goost" business does it. We can see it now: Bergen Evans leading a revival, with Brooks Atkinson at the trombone.

Really, men, you have it all wrong. Clarity is not a threat. "I would rather speak five intelligible words, for the benefit of others as well as myself, than thousands of words in the language of ecstasy" (I Cor. 14:19). Whoops! That's N.E.B.!

Crusaders'
Key

These typed notes, left on the lectern by a speaker at the Circle Writing Anti-Communism Crusade, were picked up by the janitor and handed to one of our southwest operatives:

1. Thank the generals for being here tonight. Comfort them with Scripture (Deut. 25:4; I Cor. 9:9; I Tim. 5:18: "Thou shalt not muzzle the ox that treadeth out the corn").

2. Did we provide galoshes or foot shawls for the little old ladies in tennis shoes?

3. Look poor and unaffected. Don't let *U.S. News and World Report* or any other leftist magazine accuse us of looking rich and profiteering. Remember to put a forelock of hair over brow.

4. Remember sponsor. Community sing: "Praise God from whom oil blessings flow."

5. Don't name opponents. Avoid libel. Don't say which ministers turn communists. Let it be thought that most of them do.

6. Sound literate. Quote Ayn Rand. Use big words when discussing Marxism. They're bored about this part anyhow.

7. Announce: Autographed copies of *You Can't Trust the Reader's Digest* (in condensation) are for sale.

8. If any bombs go off tonight, have prepared statement ready, disclaiming association therewith. [*Penciled in at this point: "Don't forget to pay the hecklers if we can find them after our police throw them out. Thank the police."*]

9. Dissociate self from Birch Society. [*Penciled in: "Wire Robert Welch that we're misquoted in tomorrow's paper."*]

10. Ask if librarians, Methodist ministers, schoolteachers are in audience; ask if they've taken loyalty oaths. If not, why not?

11. Watch language. Refer to "red" and "blue" herrings alike.

12. There are no white herrings in our business.

13. Give people something to do. Meet criticism of fanaticism. Tell them how to organize pickets in front of churches. Include books in bonfires at high school pep rallies. Urge churches to get out of NCC. Ask them to give to our crusade.

14. Mumble at times; stumble over words. Work on audience sympathy; get them to identify.

15. Tell them that hot new joke about Adlai Stevenson.

16. Also the one about Cardinal Spellman. [*Crossed out.*]

17. Every once in a while say something snide about New York. [*Penciled in: "Skip this point in Long Island speech."*]

18. Link *Together* magazine, *Daily Worker,* and *Presbyterian Life.*

19. Ask if the marines present know who Ming Se Tung is. They won't. Wire Strom tomorrow.

20. Coin a new word: try "symptcoms" (people who show communist symptoms). Memorize this; it might get quoted.

21. In light of No. 9, point out that the lectern is made of birch. That will pacify his gang.

22. Tell about success of the Freedom Ball at River Island.

23. Thank movie stars for coming. (If only Lassie and Silver show up, skip this.)

24. Blue tie.

25. Ask the generals if they want to say a few words. Don't give them time to get started.

26. Count the audience so we can refute journalists tomorrow. [*Penciled in: "Count before we throw the hecklers out."*]

Soul Counting
via Eugenics

Use of the first person singular throughout this piece, and the initials at the end of it, contradict our pattern of editorial anonymity. The editors have consented to this departure from the pattern in order to give me equal time for replying to friends and foes who have been sending me newspaper clippings based on a religious wire service report headed: "Says Happy Parents Produce More Girls." These folks know that I am half a pair of parents of four boys; that I have been to date blissfully unaware of my unhappiness; that I have up my sleeve a semisecret plan whereby this little Swiss-American foursome of mine shall enter the theological lists two decades hence. My felicitous situation is threatened by that news release, so I want to share a burden with other "unhappy" (by implication) parents of sons.

It seems that the Rev. F. Schoettler of Wanuma, New Guinea, has made a scientific study of the sex ratio of births in relation to the spiritual health and happiness of the parents at the time of conception. (How does anyone *know* in what state of health and happiness parents are at the time of conception?) He finds that emotional disturbance in father and mother—their failure to follow New Testament teachings against anxiety, their inability to "cast all care upon God"—produces boys; believing, faithful, happy, relaxed parents produce girls. Arguing from this evidence, the New Guinea anthropologist-missionary concludes that the proportion of girls in a congregation is a better indicator of the spiritual health of its members than is tithing, attendance at the Lord's Supper, or the number of volunteers for church work.

I began to apply the report to myself. It is disturbing to discover that I have the problem of not knowing I had a problem. As a Christian minister I am even more embarrassed by the visibility of the proof (namely, my four sons) that I do not practice what I preach; for of course if I did practice complete faith in God, I should be the father of girls. As it is, my son-fathering colleagues and I will soon be asking the liturgical houses to supply us with chasubles with a scarlet "A" (for anxiety). To the students of ministerial crack-up, suicide, and divorce patterns, we will provide one more alarming indicator.

But I still nurse hope. Maybe Schoettler's evidence is local. Maybe, by a perverse trick, just the opposite sex ratio prevails in the circles of happiness in North America. Maybe the Mrs. and I really *were* happy all along. Maybe Schoettler's twelve-

year sampling was too time-bound, too narrow. Maybe his con-
clusions are too sweeping, too abrupt. Maybe his view of the
conception-birth continuum involves a *post hoc, ergo propter
hoc* fallacy. But none of my hopeful stabs will convince those
gloating, prideful, now-certified-to-be-happy friends of mine
who are fathers of girls.

So I have cast about for a silver lining to Schoettler's cloud,
and I have found one, *viz.:* So far this year as a pastor I have
baptized sixteen girls and eight boys. If, as Schoettler insists,
this proportion is the indicator of a congregation's spiritual
health and happiness, all is well with my people. For a considerable time I must have been bearing their unhappinesses
(or at least the unhappiness of two-thirds of them) and thus
released great happiness among them. Schoettler has opened up
an avenue of vicariousness for me. I can suffer. My negative
thinking has unleashed a flow of positive thinking in the block.
Life takes on meaning and purpose. *Now I am happy.* I have
spiritual health. But I do not intend, I do not hope, to provide
Pastor Schoettler with any future empirical data to verify this
mood!

M.E.M.

Famous
Last Words

In his introduction to Barnaby Conrad's lively collection of
Famous Last Words, Clifton Fadiman describes a parlor game
in which people invent possible last words for their friends.
(For example, "Mike Wallace: *Now, Sir, you once said in
Genesis . . .*") But why bother thinking up untried originals?
Why not borrow tried and true ones from famous people of the
past? A few minutes of rummaging in Conrad's book brought
these possible borrowings to mind:

If the end comes on Tuesday (press day), our staff could say:
"How much longer will it last? I had some important things to

attend to" (originally, King Victor Emmanuel II to his doctor). For our many friends we have other ideas. A denominational bureaucrat could try Adam Smith's *"I believe we must adjourn the meeting to some other place."* After the "Peale group" meeting in Washington in 1960, the Marble Collegiate clergyman might well have memorized for future use the dying motto of Death Valley Scotty: *"I got four things to live by: Don't say nothin' that will hurt anybody. Don't give advice—nobody will take it anyway. Don't complain. Don't explain."*

The John Birch Society could borrow from Alexander Pope's word to his doctor: *"I'm dying, sir, of a hundred good symptoms."* Misanthropes of the radical right could expose their motives in the words of Carl Panzram, executed in 1930: *"I wish the whole human race had one neck and I had my hands around it."* (They probably would exempt the suburban 8 P.M. filmstrip viewers.)

Senator Barry Goldwater, never quite sure which century he is living in, could take Richelieu's words about the coming French Revolution: *"What would Louis XIV have said!"* Or Richard Nixon, with an eye on 1968, could to those who thought him politically dead quote from the French poet Paul Verlaine who said, when he heard friends discussing his approaching death, *"Don't sole the dead man's shoes yet."*

Jimmy Hoffa could turn to Walter White for his last words; when White's wife asked how White liked his daughter's manner of dress, his last words were, *"I plead the Fifth Amendment."* An anti-American Medical Association man, critical of doctors' fees, could learn from Thomas Paine. Paine's doctor said, *"Your belly diminishes";* replied the dying Paine, *"And yours augments."* Sherman Adams, remembering the heat of a vicuna coat, could draw on the words of Stanislas I of Poland (as he died of burns received when his bathrobe caught fire): *"You gave it to me to warm me, but it has kept me too hot."* Horace Traubel, friend of Walt Whitman, said, *"Look, Flora . . . just over the rocks there . . . quick!"* His wife replied, *"I don't see anyone."* This could serve for those who chance to look, unforewarned, on a fifty-megaton bomb explosion not enough hundreds of miles away. Right-wing billionaire Harold Hunt could take William Vanderbilt's *"I have had no real gratification or enjoyment of any sort more than my neighbor on the next block who is worth only half a million."* Nikita Khrushchev, anticipating his place in the Lenin-Stalin mausoleum, could use Vespasian's *"Ut puto, deus fio"* (I suppose I am now becoming a god).

Readers who buy and read Conrad, or who can devise other parallels, might try their hand and send us a few. We do not promise to print *all* we receive, but some just might do.

Angels and Gargoyles

This summer we find our thoughts turning again and again to angels. Lest you, dear reader, find such a turning singularly uncharacteristic, we add that we have also found gargoyles crossing our mind. The vision of angels haunts us every time we see a picture of the President of the United States in the papers or on TV. We have not yet recovered from the news that his face looks out from an altar panel that has been gracing the Vatican for a number of years. It is the face he wore twenty-three years ago when he posed for Irena Wiley, sculptress of the panel, who mounted his visage on the body of an angel; but they are still unmistakably the Kennedy lineaments. The vision of gargoyles haunts us whenever we think of Eusebius Church in Arnhem, Holland. The church, an eleventh-century Gothic structure which was badly damaged in World War II, is being restored, and the restorers have been giving the Gothic gargoyles a twentieth-century look. Among the immortalized symbols which scandalize some Hollanders: Donald Duck, Mickey Mouse, and the face of a clergyman who doesn't go along with the idea of modernizing Gothic.

Glancing through the week's news, we were inspired to pick

a few angels and gargoyles to decorate our (hypothetical) cathedral. The gargoyles are easier. For example, right on the door we would have the face of Erwin Iserloh, the kill-joy Roman Catholic historian at Trier, Germany, who is trying to prove that Martin Luther did not nail the ninety-five theses to the sixteenth-century church door, but merely fired them off, air mail special delivery, to two of his superiors. If the professor is right, we shall have some pretty dull Reformation pageants this year—no "hammer blows heard round the world." We propose to carve the head of Dr. Iserloh with a hammer poised, sword-of-Damocles style, above it.

On both sides of our (hypothetical) cathedral door we want statues. One will be a replica of the "Monument to Faithful Darkies" which we just learned was set up in Louisiana years ago. Opposite it we shall have an original "Monument to Faithless Whities." But soaring above this there will be an angelic figure bearing the face of Frances O. Kelsey, who spotted the dangers in the drug, thalidomide. This Kelsey angel will be shown trampling underfoot two finny infants, symbolizing the reckless medicos who experiment with suspicious drugs on human beings.

We shall also have a few gargoyles appropriate to the age of automation. One will be a celestial mathematician transfixed with a hyphen, to memorialize the party who forgot the hyphen in an equation fed to the recent Venus-bound rocket. That error misled the missile and led to its destruction. The cost: $18,000,000. Our cathedral is to cost $300,000; so the rocket money would take care of building sixty cathedrals. Then we shall have a witty, grinning, cynical gargoyle to represent the hoaxer who sold a "microdynameter," guaranteed to diagnose any illness, to scores of medical quacks at a fancy price. When tested the machine produced what must be some sort of sign of the times: "It gave the same diagnosis for a dead man as for a living one." On the spire of our cathedral will be a rotating replica of Telstar, supported by an eternally spinning statue of the joker whose idea of good programing was to put a Chicago Cubs baseball game on camera for European consumption.

We began by saying we have thought much about angels lately. Readers worried about this lofty trend can relax: we have found only one angel for our cathedral, but of gargoyles we have found plenty.

3 Religious Intelligence

The Religious
Intelligencer

People really "in the know" in the field of religion are talking about evidences of religious vitality in our blessed land. For instance:

In advertising its cruises the Holland-America Line trumpets: "Take your pick of scores of fun activities." Among those listed are "Cocktail Lounges, Captain's Champagne Parties, Professional Nightclub Revues, Gin Rummy Tournaments, Night Owl Clubs, Tea Dansants, Jousting Contests"—and, finally, "Religious Services." (Art thou weary, art thou nervous? Try H-A's religious service.)

A recent advertisement for "beautiful, jewelled silver crosses" beams itself first to "those to whom the cross has a deep religious significance." But, not wishing to miss any segment of the market, it goes on: "Even for those who are not as deeply religious, this pendant is a beautiful, tasteful, delicate piece of jewelry which will be treasured by its owner and admired by all who see it." (*See* John 12:32.)

The Mystic Arts Book Society lists among its "mystic" titles *Amulets and Talismans, Phantasms of the Living,* and—yes— *Jesus.*

A press release from Duke University tells us that the school's athletes recently met together for their annual "Brawny Beef with Bibles" church service. Forecasters note: Duke may be headed for a losing season, judging by the inside tip given in the prayer offered by Johnny Markas (" 'Greek' to his buddies, and 200 pounds of superbly-conditioned grid star . . ."): "Strengthen us for those dark days which may be before us . . ."

29

Methodist District Superintendent Dean E. Richardson of Buffalo repealed everything since second-century astronomer Ptolemy when he announced that his district is being mapped from the air "so we will see it in somewhat the same way the good Lord sees it."

The heavens opened up and sent down rain for the first running of the Winona Christian Olympics at Winona Lake, Indiana, August, 1962. Despite the drenching and slow track, winners emerged, each of whom received a medal inscribed "So Run to Obtain."

In revising its blue laws the Massachusetts legislature accidentally let a measure permitting dancing on Sunday slip by. "There'll be plenty of red faces over this," said one legislator; "I thought we had killed that section."

From a seminary newsletter we received this corrective to commerce, in verse:

> On some crepe paper moss lay an old chocolate cross,
> With a sign, "Won't you buy one or two?"
> On its fresh cellophane was this happy refrain,
> "Only Ten Cents and So Good for You."
> So please dig down and buy one today,
> For it's in the American Way.
> Celebrate Eastertide, it's got peanuts inside.
> All through Lent you'll be happy and gay.

There's more, but this gives you the idea.

Escape-Hatch Religion

Americans are, we have perceived, in every way religious. But they like to have escape alleys in their avenues of altars. For instance, in a recent "Religious Remarkables," a syndicated filler page for the religious press, we noted the following remarkable statement: "GENERAL STONEWALL JACKSON WOULD

NOT FIGHT ON SUNDAY"—and then in small type: "if he could possibly help it." We nominate St. Stonewall as the patron saint of America's religious escape-hatchers.

Until recently there seemed to be no architectural expression for this penultimate kind of interest in ultimates. Now we have found it; if you write to the *Chicago Sun-Times,* Box 992, G.P.O., New York City, and ask for Design B-57—and enclose fifty cents—you will get a set of blueprints for an almost but not quite inescapably religious home. Here are excerpts from a *Sun-Times* blurb describing the "home with a religious heart":

> . . . Into every home he hopes to sell, today's builder crowds as much material splendor as possible for the lowest possible cost because that is the success formula proven by experience.
>
> The formula neglects one factor being emphasized in thousands of churches at this season of the year: Man does not live by bread alone. Rising church membership in the United States indicates that many Americans are disillusioned by a completely material life and are turning to religion to find a deeper meaning to their existence.
>
> But as every clergyman will take pains to explain, religion has no real benefit if its practice is confined to a trip to church a couple [of] times a year. The faithful of every creed are exhorted to take their religion to heart and make it a part of the fabric of daily life.

The author calls this an "unusual prelude" to House of the Week B-57, a unique split-level which puts religion into architecture "by providing a tiny chapel in the home." "It isn't an afterthought. . . . It was in the plan from the beginning [that has a Genesis or Johannine ring, doesn't it?] and even has the traditional shape of a church, a symbolic cross." (What would Jews do?) Then the blurbist relaxes us a bit by reminding us that architect Rudolph A. Matern, no bluenose, didn't "neglect the material in providing for the spiritual." All is there in split-level splendor; there is even a theological note: a "liberal use of brick," a "gracious appearance."

Now let us look at the blueprint's small print. Sure enough, in cruciform ostentation the plans provide for a PRIVATE CHAPEL 8 ft. 3 in. by 9 ft. 2 in.—but our suspicious eyes follow the arrow leading to a note saying: "alternate studio, den, sewing room, etc." This escape clause takes all the zing and zest out of an otherwise admirable plan. The religious heart in the home is but an option. You can sew, rather than kneel, in this split-level.

We might "fence the tables" at communion—but we want a gate. We might hit the sawdust trail—if it cushions our feet and leads to a back door. We might engage in combat, but never on Sunday—unless absolutely necessary. We might build a house designed to include a chapel—but at the last minute we can, thanks to the spirit of St. Stonewall, the plans of architect Matern, and the American escape clause rationale, still find Freudian enhousement in a cruciform den.

A Klenzer
for Your Soul

The Judaeo-Christian tradition is in real trouble in the piety of America. Evidences of this fact reach us every week—so many that we could easily compile an anthology of them. We might call this anthology "Inversions"; popular religion so often seems to give a 180-degree turn to the things that should be heard in church or synagogue. Forthwith, two samples from our projected anthology.

Sample No. 1. We all know the phrase "cleanliness is next to godliness"—a copybook maxim that is virtually granted canonical status in America. The following is a soapy "godliness is next to cleanliness" inversion, from the pages of a Sunday church bulletin (the original source is a Kiwanis Committee on Support of Churches in Their Spiritual Aims):

"DUZ you DREFT along with the TIDE? VEL, now is the

time to CHEER up. If you want JOY, the TREND is to BREEZE along to church on Sunday morning. But too many WOODBURY their heads in a pillow and remain in bed, or work to make their house SPARKLE, forgetting that the Lord's Day was made for LESTOIL. But when the Lord is given first consideration, a DOVE will never have to send an S.O.S. 4 U who put Almighty God last, trusting to LUX, and who intend to miss church again this Sunday, maybe someone ought to DIAL you to remind you of the IVORY palaces up yonder. This is not a silly BABO worship; it is intended to AD to your LIFEBUOY. So next Sunday dress up SPIC AND SPAN and DASH like a COMET to God's house. Then as you sing PRAISE to God, you will get a wonderful KLENZER for your soul."

Sample No. 2. No doubt you have heard that love of money is the root of all evil; and that you cannot serve both God and mammon. But now you can discover that God *is* mammon. All you have to do is to order an Inner Sanctum Wallet from Aristocrat Leather Products, Inc., New York City. With it you will receive a pamphlet titled *Secrets of Successful People*. After quoting the usual advice from Horatio Alger and Thomas Edison, the Aristocrat pamphlet gets to the point. The greatest enemy of success is fear. "How do you conquer fear? Some of our foremost business leaders have overcome fear by faith and a strong belief in God. Others by sheer will power." Then comes the therapy: "Keep a large bill, a ten or a twenty or a fifty, in the secret compartment of the Inner Sanctum Wallet where others cannot see it. Inner Sanctum Wallets are ideal for this purpose. . . . Having this large bill that will take care of any [sic] emergency does much toward building self-confidence. . . . How can you get self-confidence? Thousands of $10,000 salesmen, buyers, managers, executives . . . carry a ten dollar bill, or larger, tucked away in an Inner Sanctum Wallet."

What happens to a $10.01, $20.01, or $50.01 emergency? You can always fall back on will power. You might even try God. By the way, what have *you* been reading? We need cheering.

Again and
Again and Again

Repetition leads to boredom. Boredom leads to quiet despair. Quiet despair kills. In line with our interest in promoting meaningful life, we have decided to wage war on repetition. Could not an infinite amount of time be saved humanity if, in kindergarten, children were taken aside and drilled and drilled and drilled (but we repeat!) in certain basics of life which admit of no exception and thus need no future repetition? For instance: "All characters in this film are fictitious, and . . ." Why finish the phrase? Why repeat it? Or, "All rights in this book are reserved, and the . . ." Until there are exceptions, why reiterate the whole phrase? Think of the time we would save if all the phrases that have become so timeworn as to be ignored were firmly planted once and for all in the impressionable minds of kindergarteners and then dispensed with!

What we are really leading up to is the release of energy that could come about if we would dispense with repetition in the *religious* realm. From now on, why repeat the obvious reminders we note below?

Guests are *always* declared to be welcome at churches, whether they are or not. Why say so again and again? Latecomers are *never* seated during prayers or Scripture-readings; why the Sunday bulletin asterisks that constantly remind us of this fact?

Denominational conventions are full of repetition; from year to year and from convention to convention, the pattern does not change. Thus when an official retires or is honored for long service, praise upon praise is heaped upon him and his achievement. He coyly goes along with it all and reminds those present of a few items overlooked on the mimeographed list provided. Then he *always* reminds them that he really didn't do any of it—God did it all, and he is sorry they had to point out all the items in his pedigree. We can cut down on repetition if in the future we dispense with either (1) God or (2) the rattling off of lists of achievements.

Pluralism occasions paradoxical repetitions. People involved in the competitive aspect of denominationalism periodically remind us that they are not involved in the competitive aspect of denominationalism. Rather, they argue, they are merely serving the Kingdom, and the competitive system keeps them on the jump. This repetition is caused by the particularity that needs to be universal.

Pluralism also occasions a universal that ends up being particular—and produces repetition. "I don't think it matters what a man believes, so long as he is good and sincere . . ." it begins, and then ends, "unless he is Catholic" (or Southern Baptist or Jewish or Orthodox or High Anglican—you fill in from here). Repetition bores. Boredom leads to . . . But we repeat.

Edifying Edifices

News on the religion front kept us so busy this week that we feel constrained to confine the outline of the week's shape to ecclesiastical doings. In summary:

This is the church: We hadn't found out about it until now, but in 1793 at Hop, Norway, an 800-seat church was built of papier-mâché. At first hopeful that this planned-obsolescence approach might solve our contemporary problem of bad church architecture (could not one good rain have washed the Hop church away?), we were disheartened to notice that the church lasted thirty-seven years. More durable is the new Marcel Breuer–designed church for St. John's University and Abbey in Minnesota. "Almost perfect," decrees Dean Ahti Auranen, who builds churches for the Church of Finland. We concur.

This is the steeple: On October 17 the Skyhook Lift Slab Company of Kansas City, Kansas, will lift a three-million pound dome for a Church of God edifice at Anderson, Indiana. If you are nearby, drop over—five thousand will be on hand to watch the hydraulic operation. After the dome is lifted, the walls will be built. Speaking of domes, here is news on the egghead front: degrees in religion were plentiful last year. Bachelors were up 2.2 per cent, masters 11.9 per cent, earned doctorates 4.5 per cent. Unearned doctorates we refuse to report on.

Open the door: Attractions to the religious life were many. For example, while banks in the Indian state of Kerala were failing, the "Paradise Bank, Ltd.," in the town of Alwaye, was prospering. In case Protestants of the positive-thinking school want to cash in on this prosperity, they might note that what this bank accepts as deposits is prayer cards, indicating investment of "immense treasures in the world to come." Begun nine years ago at Alwaye's Roman Catholic Apostolic Seminary, the papally blessed effort has as its aim "saving the world at large." Each year the total "spiritual income" is sent to the Pope, who "offers it to Our Lady."

And here are the people: Remember when actors used to act? In the post—Charlton Heston era, they are also expected to be theologians. Two weeks ago our editorial columns reported on the man who plays "Jesus" in *King of Kings.* Weekly now we receive spot press releases on the actors in the screen play. This week Ron Randell, who plays Lucius the Centurion, counsels us that his role "is representative of the plight of modern man." (He used to play "the sort of fellow whom the hero always describes to the girl as a nice chap but a frightful bore!")

You meet such interesting people! Matthew, Mark, Luke, and John, bless the stamp I lick upon: for the first time ever, the four evangelists grace postage stamps. The four stamps have been issued for regular use in the postal system of Switzerland.

Antonio Ordóñez, the great Spanish matador, is to sponsor a four-day retreat in Estremadura for Catholic bullfighters, impresarios, stable hands, and critics. The devotions will terminate with a bullfight. We are not *aficionados*—but then, we are Protestant—so nobody need be surprised.

A recent heaven-and-hell "Personal" in a Chicago newspaper:

"Rev. Hargrove, contact me, the Heating Man. Very important. TA 9-9427."

Spring
Cleaning

Springtime tempts us from our wonted ways. The chance to gaze through a budding tree at a brilliant sky; a loaf of bread, a jug of Pepsi, a book of Rilke, with or without a thou—these are paradise enow. But if we are to indulge in the rites of spring we must first finish our next pressing assignment, in this case providing our readers with what many editors choose to call "brief items from Religious News Service." (In other words, we have been cleaning out our desk drawers.) Without the following authenticated notices left over from winter, our weekly Pen-ultimate slant on life in the early 1960's could hardly be complete.

Pope John XXIII has named St. Bona, a twelfth-century Benedictine, as patroness of airline hostesses. The last words of this "celestial protector," we are led to surmise, must have been *"Ambrosia, potio, aut lac?"*

Charles Blase Bukovich, forty-three, is an artist whose favorite medium—mosaics composed of jagged bits of broken glass—often, so RNS reports, "makes the agony of creativity a very physical thing." In constructing the stations of the cross in Jersey City's St. Peter's Catholic Church he cut himself while at work on No. 14. He couldn't stop to bandage the wound—the concrete was hardening: "That's why, if you look closely, you can see the blood in the mosaic."

At Whitehorse, Yukon Territory, Oblate Missionary Pierre Rigaud placed second in a twenty-four-mile dog-team race. He was beaten by one Andrew Smith (no doubt a Southern Baptist).

Evangelist Billy Graham, after being cited as one of America's "best-tied men," at the suggestion of a southern fashion columnist donated a necktie to an auction benefiting a Belmont, North Carolina, Roman Catholic nursery. Said the columnist: "It could be a collector's item." We have not heard who won the ecumenical four-in-hand.

Father Joel Shevers, director of St. Therese's Chapel at the Peabody, Massachusetts, Northshore Shopping Center, appealed for old gold to fashion a new chalice. Among the gifts: a medal inscribed "New England Elbow and Collar Wrestling Championship, 1897," and a few sets of gold teeth.

Vatican authorities recently inaugurated a one-way traffic system to deal with congestion in Vatican City; they also installed the tiny principality's first traffic light. In the Vatican as in California, you can turn right on red after a full stop.

The governing body of Christ Church Cathedral (Episcopal) in St. Louis decided that the realistic figures in the panels of a controversial new cross in the memorial chapel would have to go. The fact that a St. Louis brewery and the local major league baseball team were depicted was disturbing to many. So: "The Cathedral chapter has ruled that the cross may remain, but the occupations and industries must be represented symbolically instead of realistically." We presume that instead of Stan Musial, a symbolic cardinal will be enthroned—and in an Episcopal Cathedral! Symbolic justice.

As we write, the Senate enters an anticipated ten-day filibuster. That body could well resurrect a February prayer of guest chaplain Brayne E. Driskill, asking forgiveness for time wasted.

Pass the Pepsi, pass the Rilke . . .

4 Positive Thinking

A Simple
Honorable Man

How much is that doggie in the pulpit?
The one with the publicity hound's stare?

When Dr. Stuart Hamilton Merriam introduced his German shepherd dog into the pulpit at New York's Broadway Presbyterian Church, he began the sequence of attention-getting moves which marred his ministry there. Publicity-hounding is but one of the charges brought against this clergyman by his presbytery, but it is the charge that interests us more than the others. We are unable and unwilling to intervene between scrapping Presbyterians in this regrettable and humanly expensive issue. But we do ask: What is new about a minister's serving as his own public relations expert?

Many historic instances come to mind. Jeremiah was not exactly hiding his P.R. talent when he cracked a crock as an attention-getting device to begin a sermon. Don't tell us that John Peter Gabriel Muhlenberg did not know what he was doing in 1776 when he stripped off his pulpit robe and stood before his congregation in colonel's uniform, ready to go to war. When Phillips Brooks called preaching the dispensing of "truth through personality" he knew how the personality had to be developed. Pope Urban II did not hide his flair for drama under a bushel when he preached for a crusade in 1095. Methodist Peter Cartwright was as hammy as Dr. Merriam when he offered to wrestle the infidels in his audience—and when he did.

It is second-phase Merriam that bothers us more than first-phase. Merriam not only did dramatic things; he advertised them. When present-day preachers issue their own P.R. statements, advertise sermons, indulge in gimmicks—then we become disturbed.

What a clean, pure breath of air comes from Conrad Richter's *A Simple Honorable Man*! It is a novel about a Pennsylvania preacher who ministered to what Robert Frost would call "officially unimportant people" a few decades ago, in an era that seems uncomplex compared to our own. No one noticed him. He died unknown. He left no visible stamp on history. You won't believe this of hardhearted old Pen-ultimaters, but more than one tear came to our eyes and a real warming to our heart as we read of Richter's Rev. Harry Donner—whom, incidentally, G. Elson Ruff now identifies (in the *Lutheran*) as the real-life father of Conrad Richter.

Today too, off-Broadway and down in Eveningside Depths, there are many simple, honorable men who are as much embarrassed by the antics of Dr. Merriam on Morningside Heights as by the antics of the Madison Avenue legion whom he emulates. All of us have encountered these simple, honorable men —at conferences, conventions, convocations. Young and old they are. You have not heard of them before. No bronze plaques in million-dollar churches will ever commemorate them and their work. *Newsweek* will not find them newsworthy, and *The New York Times*, while it would consider their doings "fit to print," could not call them news. But they are there, quietly witnessing and influencing, misfits for God in any generation. Alone, in prayer. With one another, in counsel. With two or three, in upbuilding. With a small circle, when the candles burn low and death is near. With pathetic but faithful little flocks.

Dr. Ruff, writing about Richter's novel, says that the author no longer goes to church. He remembers too well the "dark, theocratic cloud" that lowered over his childhood. But we have a hunch that Richter and his contemporaries would at least stand on the church's threshold, were "the simple honorable man" and not the publicity hound the dominant—if not the universal—image of the man in the pulpit today.

A Complicated
Honorable Man

Dear Simeon Stylites:

It is two years now since "Saint" was officially prefixed to your name. Only once in that time have we disturbed your peace. I am sorry to bother you again. But as you know, our contacts in your realm are few and we have to overwork our friends. I want you please to look up a reverend father of mine, Pastor O. A. Geiseman. In a phrase that would make him uneasy, he has lately "gone to his reward." You must have met him.

Now, I know a thousand other ministers must have died in November of this year. Any number of them will be reminiscing with you about the days when you used to visit St. John's-by-the-Gas-Station, the parish they *all* thought was their own. I want to single out a particular reader of yours, however. As you know, we are not highly devoted to the Cult of the Parson on this page. But we do like to take note of exceptional people, and hate to hold their habitation in parsonages against any of them.

The problem in introducing Dr. G. is twofold. On the one hand, he did not belong to the "power elites" of institutional religion; that is, while he was perhaps the best known pastor in his denomination, he was a general practitioner of the kind *Who's Who* can't bring itself to deal with. On the other hand, he had the misfortune of being pastor, for almost forty years, of a large, well-off, successful church in one of the better suburbs—River Forest, Illinois. That dooms him in the eyes of those who share the mystique of the primitive. By which I mean that we know how to revere the obscure—the "simple honorable men" of novelist Conrad Richter's depiction, or the *Cure d'Ars* type of priest. We cultivate the memory of unknown and yet well-known prison camp chaplains, martyred missionaries, inner city ministers. We have not yet learned to honor the stewardship of faithful pastors in "normal" settings.

His people knew Dr. G. as preacher, counselor, administrator, friend. I knew him as all of these, and more. As a former assistant of his when I was fresh (and I do mean *fresh*) out of seminary, I want to speak about him and his significance. And I am speaking for others who need some occasion to pay tribute to mentors, to senior clergymen whose forte it is to encourage the oncoming generation. Let Dr. G. symbolize all the clerics who without jealousy, insecurity, resentment, or condescension put heart into their juniors—prod them into advanced study, take note of their achievements, "drop their names" when that might do some good all around, counsel when necessary. If in every life there were two or three great influencers like Dr. G., that life could be marked as worth while.

Don't think of this as an obituary. (Our editor is wary of overburdening our columns with death notices.) When a kibitzer berated Dr. G.'s newest assistant for not draping his church in crepe on funeral day, an obituary-killing retort spoke for us all: "Why should we? We're celebrating the resurrection." The young pastors who, on that crisp November afternoon of resurrection, sought to minister to Dr. G.'s congregation with the fragile instrument of words, would, I am sure, join me in this memorial to one who belonged to the Fellowship of Encouragers, who read well the Author and Finisher of our faith. Keep your eye on him. He's not much on protocol. We never could quite keep track of the way you rank saints and martyrs, angels and archangels, cherubim and seraphim. But next time a skinny, intense young minister arrives up there in need of a friend, watch out: St. Dr. G. may grab him by the sleeve and whistle him past many ranks and hierarchies, right to the inner court.

Once in a while we should recall a *complicated* honorable man. Dr. G. is my first nomination.

M.E.M.

A Few of
Our Favorites

The other day we read a passage in Teilhard de Chardin's letters which, as Harry Truman would say, "hit us right where we live." The traveler-scientist-priest argued that a certain view of the real world is just as closed to many Christians as the world of faith is to unbelievers. "The Lord preserve my passion for the world and a great gentleness toward it," he wrote, "and help me to the last to be a whole man."

We are drawn to his comment, for we also desire to keep a passion for the world and gentleness toward it. "Wait! List! Halt!" cries our imaginary reader. "You Pen-ultimate people *like* something? You are always finding fault." If the letters we receive are an indicator, some of our readers feel that our pen-ultimate attachment to the world sees us finding it cold, cruel. Not so. In the Teilhardist spirit we want to out-positive-think the opposition. So here, with passion and gentleness, we set down some things to like in the world.

1. Autumn.

2. Wilma Rudolph, running.

3. Edward P. Morgan, calmly and objectively commenting on the news.

4. The Portsmouth Priory, designed by Petro Belluschi.

5. "For All the Saints"—sung loudly.

6. Stan Musial, as an athlete and as a man.

7. Vacations with children. Vacations without children.

8. Hindemith's three organ sonatas.

9. Denominational conventions, when they are over.

10. *Missa Luba,* a sort of Congolese chant version of the mass sung by Les Troubadours du Roi Baudouin.

11. Inez Robb, for surprising us and everybody, and bearding a contingent of the right wing in its Phoenix lair.

12. Days when air-raid signals break down and are silent.

13. Chinese "good luck" bamboo cricket cages with crickets in them.

14. Chinese "good luck" bamboo cricket cages after the crickets are gone.

15. Martin Luther King, Jr., for the time he refused to play the role of a Negro senator from Georgia in Otto Preminger's film version of *Advise and Consent*.

16. Rusty fallout shelter signs starting to fall down.

17. Abstract expressionist Alfred Manessier's "Crown of Thorns" or "Resurrection" (the latter in the Venice Biennale) —if you must look at abstract expressionism.

18. Representative John V. Lindsay (R., N.Y.), for declaring that President Kennedy ought to give the people the facts about contamination of milk by radioactive fallout.

19. Uncontaminated milk.

20. Lakeside retreats with a faith-full exegete expounding St. Matthew.

21. People who admit they don't like Henry Miller.

22. The literate laity.

23. Psalm 27.

24. People who write the editor and say they like our column.

25. People who write the editor and say they don't like our column.

26. The cover photography of the *Mennonite*.

27. Ministers who talk in the same tone of voice in church as outside it.

28. Boys who don't play Little League baseball.

29. White-painted wooden Methodist churches in Iowa.

30. Vespers.

The One Hundred
Least

A recent issue of *Life* contained photographs of a hundred "under forty" men and women whom the magazine labels the "most important" people of the "take-over generation"—the "red-hot hundred" who are leading the "big breakthrough" in science, art, religion, politics, and what have you. With the red-hot in mind, we climbed into our asbestos suit and, looking defensive lest we be taken over, got to work on the "important" scheme from the opposite end. Who, we asked ourselves, are the hundred *least* important people? The field is crowded. Here are some starting suggestions:

Reading an article on upgraded pastoral pay in another weekly, we came upon a statement by Dr. Merle Fish, head of Los Angeles' church federation, that "most of the fellows I know who are underpaid are incompetent. They couldn't make it any better anywhere else." That reminds us of a minister we know out in South Dakota. He has been too busy with sick calls, sermons, and his Greek New Testament to do anything about upgrading his pay. He's barely eking out an existence. There's a "least important" man for you! Probably he has never heard the Fish story.

Next on our list are two southerners: the white Georgia church member who made room for a Negro to kneel beside him during the service, and the little white girl in New Orleans who took a little Negro girl's hand on the playground. You never heard *their* names, did you?

We want to cite also an elevator man at a certain hospital who hands us a bonbon as we enter his conveyance, and *always* says, "Your pleasure is my pleasure." We do not know where he got the phrase, but we like it. And a maintenance man out at the airport who sometimes hands us a paper towel from some hidden supply in the washroom. It is his quiet refutation of that technological blunder, the "electric hand drier." Without him we never would get our hands dry. We don't know his name.

Other least-importants: The waitress who serves as if she enjoys it and still acts as if a tip is the reward for the excellence of the service. (You must know one like that somewhere, too. Think for a while. Think a bit longer.) The funeral director who talks people into unextravagant burials for their loved ones. The chap who stood against his fraternity brothers to eliminate hazing and falderal, and got the crowd to go with him to repaint a settlement house during "hell week." The high-schooler at a youth retreat we attended who quietly talked his duck-tailed boy and beehive-hairdoed girl companions out of showing off by their fortissimo playing of rock and roll. (Most of our "least importants" have a penchant for relative quiet.)

Certainly not at the head of her class is a stewardess on one of the airlines we often use. Poised, natural, she isn't overly made up and wears no pasted-on grin. Come to think of it, she is the *only* stewardess we can really remember. Likewise a church usher without the sick grin: they'll never use him for a model in the manuals on church ushering.

Often the "least importants" are children. We picture the young man working his way through college and at the same time supporting his mother. The blind child singing "This Little Gospel Light of Mine." The four grade-schoolers who regularly give up recesses to fuss over a classmate who is a muscular dystrophy victim.

It wouldn't take us long to draw up our list of one hundred least importants, but space is short. One word in our phrase keeps popping into mind: that word "least." It reminds us of something we cannot quite define and isolate. And we think of another indefinable quality that "least importants" have; you might almost call it "childlikeness." Oh, yes, now we remember: *"Of such* is the kingdom of God."

5 Liturgies and Dramas

Amen, but
Not Hallelujah

In this time of religious prosperity we have observed across the nation the closing of countless churches. Many of them have become theaters, bowling alleys, taverns, discount stores; others remain boarded up. Usually their closing occurs as the result of one of two factors: (1) Though there are more people to be served in range of the towers than there were previously, the newcomers are nonwhite. (2) Increasingly, superhighways knife their way through the cities and carve up church parishes.

We have mused upon the fact that such churches, once dedicated and consecrated to holy use, have not been deconsecrated. With a sense of propriety and concern for the holy, we consulted our Division on Liturgical Studies. The division, after finding that Big Sister Church has an order for deconsecration but that Little Brother churches haven't, devised the nice little liturgy given below. It shall be promulgated as part of Our Priceless Liturgical Heritage and shall be regarded as traditional, effective next Sunday. Appropriately, it shall be printed on parchment in Old English type.

Order for the Deconsecration of a Church

Invocation: In the name of the Great Architect of the Grand Universe and this once Grand Structure.

People: Amen, but not Hallelujah.

Collect: O Someone in the Great Somewhere who hears our every word, hear us as we deconsecrate this building, once set aside to holy use. We know that Thy ways are mysterious and

47

past finding out: therefore we shall not seek to understand Thy hand in the rendering of this noble edifice to obsolete status. We resent Thee for this; help us to hide our resentments. Bless us in our new home in the suburbs. Keep the community there from deteriorating, as this is Thy will for us. Why was it not Thy will for us here? (*At this point all religious symbols are removed.*)

Alternate Rubrics:

1. *For the Coming of the Colored People*

O Man Upstairs, we built this edifice to Thy glory and we paid for it with the work of our hands. If only Thou wouldst come down from Thy celestial rocker and visit man, Thou wouldst know how inconvenient and expensive this move is. Then Thou wouldst not have let the Negroes move in. We know that Thou hast made of one blood all the children of men and that they are all all right. In their place.

All: They are all all right. In their place. Amen.

2. *For Superhighways*

O He who holds the whole world in His hands, look upon us who stand in the sound of the bulldozer and the shadow of the toppling apartment. Do not let us get hit by any falling bricks. Bless those who will soon operate a Gas Station here, so that something can be made of this circumstance.

All: Bless us, too, who worship Thee in truth and spirit, as we go our way.

Benediction: This edifice has now been deconsecrated. Go forth once again into the world knowing that no Holy Object will be stained by Other Kinds of People and no Holy Edifice will be shaken by destructive and re-creative forces. Go in peace.

All: Yea, in the peace that passeth understanding. Amen, but not Hallelujah.

Children Must Play

The United States set off a thermonuclear explosion high over Johnston Island in the Pacific . . . [it] produced probably the most spectacular, far-flung effects of any man-made event in history.—The New York Times, July 10, 1962.

SCENE ONE

Child: Daddy, can I have the hammer and tools and some wood, to make an airplane or something?

Father: No, you're too young. That would be hard for you to do.

Child: I want to try anyhow. May I?

Father: Oh, all right. The tools are on the shelf and there is some old wood in the box underneath. Go ahead.

(Noises are heard in background. Sounds of industry and frustration are heard intermittently with the sound of hammering.)

Child (entering excitedly): Look, daddy! I couldn't make an airplane! But look what I *can* make! I can make a cross!

SCENE TWO

Child A: What's that you're playing with?

Child B: A top.

Child A: Where'd you get it?

Child B: It fell out of an envelope in the back of the book my Dad brought home tonight.

Child A: Let me see it!

Child B: No, it's mine! See how light the blue is when it spins into the white part?

Child A: Stop it! I still want to see it. It doesn't look like a top to me. There's printing on it, and you can't read. Give it to me; I want to read it. I don't think you're supposed to have it.

Child B: Oh, all right. Here it is. But you give it right back!

Child A (picking out words with effort): "Nu-clear Bomb E-ffects

Com-put-er. Revised edi-tion, 1962. Produced by J. B. Carr-oll Co., Chicago 12, Illinois." Look, I don't think you're supposed to have it.

Child B: But it's just a top, and it's my toy. I want it! Don't tell my Daddy! What else does it say?

Child A: It has some dials on it. You are supposed to set this one like this and this one like this and then "read answers in window" on the dial. Say, this is just like reading a pedometer!

Child B: What does it say?

Child A: Oh, I don't know what it means. In this window, when you set the two dials, it says: "Probable bio-log-ical effect: 1–99% ruptured eardrum; threshold lung hemorr . . . hemorr-hage; 1–99% mortality." I can't figure it out. It has more numbers on it than Dad's slide rule. It sure would be a good toy. I wish I had seen it first.

Child B: Give it back! I found it first, and I get to play with it. It's mine! Anyway, it's just a top. But it's a beautiful one!

. . . Hawaiians, who had waited for more than a month for a front-row view of the Johnston Island nuclear test shot, were rewarded with a spectacular view. . . . The most fortunate observers were those on the heights overlooking Honolulu. . . . Scientists . . . were amazed at the intensity of the long-range effects.—Ibid.

Spiritual Notebook

Friday: Picked up this card in my hotel room: "Need Spiritual Vitamins? Call Dial-a-Devotion. Phone 743–0424. When out of town, call 211–420–743–0424. If it is busy, call 211–420–743–0425." Did not need Spiritual Vitamins.

Saturday: Returned to home town. Was lonely. Needed Spiritual Vitamins. Dialed a devotion. Heard this message: "This is a recorded message. Today is Saturday. For weekend Spiritual Vitamins, Dial-a-Devotion suggests you go to church. Your Denominational Distribution Center will guide you. See the Yellow Pages." Looked up DDC in Yellow Pages. Phoned DDC. Heard this message: "This is a recorded message. Today all inquiries are being dispatched to First Protestant Church, 11:00 A.M. Sunday services."

Sunday: Still lonely. Followed Dial-a-Devotion's and DDC's suggestions. Went to First Protestant Church. At outside doors passed under closed-circuit television camera. At inner sanctuary doors took a ticket extended to me by the click of a machine. The ticket said: "Our observers on television note that you are a newcomer. We have recorded your picture for our files. You are assigned number 40697 7042 B 308110. Your IBM card will be ready at Coffee Fellowship Time this noon. Sit in Pew 4 C." Service began. Music was John Cage's "Aleatory Prelude No. 17," electronically produced, taped, and broadcast. Minister being away for the weekend, his sermon was played on tape. Topic: "The Christian Church: Resource Center for Authentic Personhood and Human Social Values." Minister acknowledged help for the sermon in church bulletin: "Thanks to Memory-O-Matic, 4205 37th Street, Brentwood, Maryland." Offering time. Was handed three-year pledge card, 156 blank checks, 156 stamped envelopes, "so that you can have the warm sense of participation even when absent."

Sunday noon: Decided to enroll child in Sunday school. Went to inquire. Filled out application, placed it in slot, waited. The responding tape said: "Bring Child 40697 7042 B 308110, Jr., to Nursery Class 97B, Tier 2, Stall 8, Wing 3 South, Parking Lot C, next Sunday 9:45 A.M." Noted house phone promising answers on any subject. Dialed "Adult Education." Was advised by recorded message to come to a session on Bonhoeffer's *Life Together* Tuesday 8 P.M.; material would be presented on closed-circuit TV via a teaching machine.

Sunday afternoon: Fellowship hour. Put money in Coffee, Hot Soup, Cellophaned Sandwich vending machines. Saw a movie on mass evangelism. Was invited to attend a rally.

Sunday night: Attended rally. Was Attendant No. 18423, Decision No. 424.

Tuesday: Received notice that Decision Card No. 424, when filed with First Protestant IBM card 40697 7042 B 308110, crumpled the latter. Was asked to come to church Thursday, at 8:00 P.M., to straighten out the matter.

Thursday: Went to straighten out trouble. Found that trouble often happens, that IBM card gets bent when another card is inserted with it in file. A *person* told me so, in person.

Friday: Arranged to have some sort of extra card inserted in file every week, so that I have to go in every Thursday, at 8:00 P.M., to straighten out the matter. With a person.

Rickety
Rickety Ree

When St. Paul made metaphorical use of athletic activities in describing his spiritual conditioning he introduced a most unfortunate precedent for his lesser followers. Cheap exhortations to the moral life, couched in the terminology of athletics, have resounded from many pulpits. Ever since the sports world got religion a few years ago, equal embarrassments have resounded from that side. Take this illustration: Bill Orwig, Indiana University athletic director, recently won the Pop Warner Award for the football "huddle prayer of the year." Remember, this is *first* prize. Some must have been worse.

> Dear Lord, as we huddle here,
> Help us all to see it clear
> That playing hard and playing fair,
> Is what we are asking everywhere.
> And as we go forth to play the game
> In sports or life, it's all the same,
> We hope to win like all the rest,
> But especially, help us, Lord, to do our best.

Our translation of what is really going on in the huddle:

> Dear Lord, as we huddle here,
> Help us all to make it clear
> That bashing teeth and pulling hair
> Is tough with helmets everywhere.
> So as we go forth to play the game,
> Help us to grab and twist and maim;
> We hope to win and then to rest
> As we tell the world which blades are best.

But there are still possibilities in athletic metaphor. The Aurora, Illinois, *Beacon-News* for January 2 reports this advance in the Kingdom: "St. Paul's freshman Walther League cheerleaders took the second place trophy at the 'Chicagoland All Lutheran Basketball-Cheerleading Tournament . . .' "

Faithful reader, we can make the best things of the worst times, and we can even rescue Sacred Cheerleading to holy causes. Why waste it in interfaith rivalries such as that between the basketballers of the Church of the Deformation and the Church of the Inarticulate Construction? Think how advantageous other uses might be. While our interfaith dialogists utter the gentilities, and our ecumenical spokesmen give and take in friendly spirit, their cheering sections could give utterance to lurking hostilities.

Examples: While the Protestant spokesmen deal in new ways with the Orthodox, the home front can cheer—may we borrow from Aristophanes and Yale?—

> Brekekekex ko-ax, ko-ax,
> Calvin, Luther, Cranmer, Knox,
> Give it to the Orthodox!

Catholic-Protestant dialogue generally proceeds around the tables of gentlemen. But from the gallery might come:

> Rickety rickety ree,
> Hit 'em in the knee;
> Rickety rickety rummick,
> Kick 'em in the etc.

Intra-Protestant relations could be exposed, too. Take this one:

> Themistocles, Themostocles, the Peloponnesian War,
> X^2, Y^2, H_2SO_4
> Who for? Why for? Episcopalians, that's who!

Votes for first prize respectfully solicited.

An Enthusiastic Correspondence

The Bunnies of the Chicago Playboy Club, through the Foster Parents Plan, have adopted 23 destitute children from countries around the world. . . . The youngsters receive $15 a month each. . . . The Chicago Bunny staff received case histories . . . giving them a basis for enthusiastic correspondence.—A December, 1962 release.

To: Kim Kin
  How Long Orphan Farm, How Long Olord, Korea

Dear Kim: I take my pen in hand to write (ha! ha!) an enthusiastic correspondence. I hope you got my $15.00 which will give you school and medicines and food for December—and clothes too, cause a girl has just gotta have nice clothes. I know you will appreciate it as it took me two hours to earn it. All of us bunnies thought it would be good at this season of peace on earth and good will to men to write you and tell you about the American Way of Life and our part in it.

I work in a club where people enter with a key and have a lot to eat and drink and they pay for it with the key and they leave. Most of the time the people are men. They carry little plastic cards instead of money. They can buy things with these cards, and then they do not have to pay taxes on them. I bring them their drinks. They don't dare touch me. I work very hard and earn $15,000 a year. A school teacher in America may only earn $4,000, but she gets to sit down more of the time. I wear a tail which makes it hard to sit down, even if I ever would get time.

Don't you wish you had a club for bunnies in Korea? But you cannot have them because they are part of the American Way of Life. Sometimes when my feet hurt I go over to the man who plays the piano and I put my head on his piano and we talk about very deep things. Then I get to thinking that what I am doing is sort of a religious thing, and I feel better. I help spread good will to men. Ministers do not like us; they call us priestesses of a new religion. But the Great Hugh, our wonnerful high priest, says they are all a bunch of blew noses, any how, the same as your Presbeterians in Korea. He (I am still speaking about Hugh) says that after all God made women and so if we become bunnies and take all our clothes off for a picture that is the most beautiful religion in God's creation. We invite ministers to join our clubs and come to our temples.

When the men leave they leave their offerings on the table. That is how I get my money. It reminds me of when I was a Babtist, and we were suppose to tithe, only now I get a tithe and a half. The average offering is $1.70, which is as much as these men give at their churches in a year to send overseas. So you can see they believe more in our religion than theirs, says the piano player. When they come in I say, "I am your bunny." But we do not talk much and cannot go away with them and in general live as if we were in a convent. I imagine it is much like your orphan farm (ha! ha!). Sometimes we are on television and we are suppose to laugh when a comedian says something. Otherwise we do not say much.

If you grow big maybe you can come to America. Pray that you grow big in front especially and if you can have the operation that doesn't make your eyes so slanty you can join our religion and worship the creation and be a bunny and spread the American Way of Life and good will to men and Merry Christmas.

I am your bunny.
BUNNY FOSTER

Nonprayers for New Yorkers

The recitation of a twenty-two-word nonliturgical, nondoctrinal, nonsectarian prayer addressed to a nondenominational God has been disallowed by the Supreme Court. The historic decision concerning a New York practice has prompted spirited controversy, but almost no one has expressed concern about filling the gap opened up in the day's schedule by abandonment of the prayer. Some have suggested that students and teachers give the time to silent meditation. Our suggestion is of a more active kind. Herewith we offer a selection of twenty-two-word (or thereabouts) nonprayers—since reference to the Deity offends the court—which New York children might ponder. It is our hope that all parents, whatever their attitude or persuasion, will find among these nonprayers one or more that they consider suitable for their children's use.

1. Happy are ye, Felix Frankfurter and Byron "Whizzer" White, that ye did not have to participate in the Supreme Court's controversial decision!

2. Vouchsafe us the wisdom to see why people who want church and state separate financially holler loudest when they are separated actually.

3. Succor us who once used the time it takes to recite twenty-two words for sharpening pencils, going to the washroom, or drinking a cola.

4. Grant that everyone concerned may cool off a bit before shooting off his mouth further on a complicated question of church and state.

5. Give us the insight to discern whether the clergyman who wrote the original Pledge of Allegiance—which did *not* include the phrase "under God"—was an atheist or a Communist.

6. Now that our fathers are fighting the Supreme Court decision and cussing out the President, we would know whether this means that we have to pray at home.

7. O ye Nikita Khrushchevs, praise ye the Earl Warrens and William O. Douglases who are doing your work—says my angry daddy.

8. Did we acknowledge our three-syllable "dependence" or our four-syllable "dependency" in the New York prayer? I can't find out from the dictionaries.

9. Guide us to an understanding of why the New York Board of Regents should have established itself as a liturgical council in any circumstance.

10. Quench our thirst to find out why southern politicians who won't let God's children (colored) into certain schools want God's name used there.

11. Aid us to discover how so many Christian clergymen became constitutional authorities overnight; did they really read the decision?

12. We beg that the American Civil Liberties Union, the Unitarian-Universalist churches, the rabbis, the ethical culturists, be not too, too happy.

13. We yearn to know what harm our little twenty-two-word prayer did as we began the school day. On second thought, what good did it do?

14. Nullify the nullifiers, lest we be again made to yawn through twenty-two uninspired words at the beginning of each school day.

To Quote
Tillich . . .

A sermon, says Bishop Gerald Kennedy, is something a minister will cross the country to deliver but will not cross the street to hear. But we keep hearing sermons. The laic and cleric listeners alike on our staff bring back from Protestant pulpits in range of their forays sounds of many sermons. Some of the sounds are not altogether pleasant. We all used to wince at chestnuts from the Victorian quotables—Spurgeon comes to mind. But we have no-

ticed that the *avant-garde* is just as predictable. If *you* have col-
lected any hackneyed allusions or illustrations, any name-drop-
pings or mannerisms from the sermons of *au courant* strivers,
send us a list. If they irritate us, too, we shall print them; the
rest we shall use to paper the walls of the *Pulpit* office. Be sure
to use indirect quotes, as preachers do. It saves writing authors
and publishers for permission.

Meantime, we give you a sample all-purpose sermon, worth a
number of ho-hums and at least a score of winces:

Dear Brethren: Hell is other people. This astute observation
by a character in a Jean-Paul Sartre play has struck me as an apt
description of our religious situation. Ever since Nietzsche announced the death of God, we have seen this assertion to be a
motif of the age of anxiety, to use Auden's phrase. It depicts
the rejection of the quest for authentic existence in the thrown-
ness (I am sorry that Heidegger's *Geworfenheit* does not trans-
late better) of finitude. Was it not occasioned by the distin-
tegration of a world view? Is not this what John Donne meant
when he said, " 'Tis all in Peeces, all coherence gone"? Or
what Yeats meant in his immortal "the centre cannot hold"?

Yet, to revert to Donne, no man is an island, as Hemingway
liked to remind us; and the man who has reverence for life, as
the Saint of Lambaréné speaks of it, will not be content to be
driven into the pathetic *Waiting for Godot* situation which
Samuel Beckett describes. There are, after all, affirmations. Is
not this what Kierkegaard meant when he quoted Shakespeare,
"Better well hung than ill wed"? That is not a whole philosophy
of life, but it is the first harbinger. There are others; the bread
and wine before us (you will recall Ignazio Silone's affirmative
use of this title), which follow the sermon, can help. Or, to
quote Graham Greene—or is it Mauriac? (it was some Catholic
or other—not Waugh; I hate Waugh)—"the grace of God is the
glue."

On all sides we see rejections, however, of this authenticity.
Ayn Rand's selfishness, Bill Buckley's conservatism—these are
signs on the campus. Is not such rejection behind Albert Camus
(a saint who did not know he was Christian) and his sports-car

death? Or Elizabeth Taylor's erotic vagrancy? Is not this the danger in David Riesman's *The Lonely Crowd?* Certainly, Mr. Riesman is correct when he calls us from other-directedness. But he, of course, cannot be kerygmatic; he cannot speak of agape. Yet someone must. If, to quote Tillich, the new being is to break through; if radical monotheism, to recall H. Richard Niebuhr's book title, is to hold sway, then we must all forsake the idols of our contemporary life. Otherwise we shall be the decent, godless people of T. S. Eliot's reference—our only monument the asphalt roads and a thousand lost golf balls. We must affirm and authenticate, or our lives, unlike this sermon, will end not with a bang but a whimper. Amen. Shall we pray?

Reformation Pageant, R.S.V.

American Protestants have long sensed a barrenness in their liturgical year. Not much of a dramatic or colorful nature happened ecclesiastically between Mother's Day and Thanksgiving Day. October 31, the Festival of the Reformation, was gradually coming to fill the gap. And, since every festival needs a gimmick—Easter eggs, Christmas trees, etc.—this one called for a rally featuring a militant, noisy church service, complete with visual aids, trumpet blasts, and, above all, a pageant. The pageant, our reading of metropolitan newspapers suggests to us, more often than not was called something like "The Hammer Blows Heard Round the World."

The formula for the pageant was simple: Rent an auditorium (a big one: this is to be a Protestant union service), a tonsure-wig, a cowl, and a monk's robe. Find a man to put in the robe. (Since the man is to play Martin Luther, it is a question whether he should be a skinny young monk, *à la* Cranach's portrait, or a rotund, beery type, as in the pictures of the mature Luther.) Also acquire a hammer and a couple of nails and a piece of parchment on which Luther's Ninety-Five Theses are lettered. Finally, make a mock-up of a church door. At the high point of the drama the chorus would sing "A Mighty Fortress," and the monk would take hammer, nails, and parchment and step up to the church door. The crowd would strain to hear the Hammer Blows Heard Round the World.

This year, doubts have been raised about such pageants. Professor Erwin Iserloh, of the University of Trier (a Catholic, wouldn't you know!), says the church-door bit is all a legend. He demythologizes the whole event and says Luther posted his theses to ecclesiastical and political leaders through the mails. German evangelicals are fighting back, and, judging from a careful article in a recent issue of *Christ und Welt*, will have the best of it on the basis of documentation. But this week we have to be ecumenical and give Dr. Iserloh and the Catholics a sporting chance. Until the matter is settled, we propose dropping the noisy pageant and substituting one which might begin something like this (the show must go on):

How the Reformation Began

TIME: Allhallows Eve, October 31, 1517.
PLACE: The Wittenberg, Germany, Post Office.

Act One

POSTMASTER: Ah, brother Martin, I'm glad to see you are mailing early. The Christmas card rush will start soon. We haven't seen you lately.

LUTHER: Writer's cramp has been bothering me. It's hard to write ninety-five theses in Old English lettering on this crumbly parchment. And then I had to make duplicates. I am going to start a Reformation.

POSTMASTER: Well, it's time we gave you Protestants equal time. Ever since that Dominican fellow named Tetzel went into the mail-order business we've been swamped with indulgences being shipped all over. The POGU for separation of church and state is all excited. They're lobbying for new postal rates on religious propaganda.

LUTHER: I hope they don't win until I get this batch of theses out. Oh, these two have to go Special Delivery Air Mail Registered.

POSTMASTER: I can't read your writing.

LUTHER: This is to Bischof Hieronymus Schulz von Brandenburg, and that one to Albrecht von Mainz—he's an archbishop.

POSTMASTER: What's that you're hiding under your robe?

LUTHER (*embarrassed*): Oh, that? That's nothing. That's just a hammer. I wanted to nail the original to the Castle Church door.

POSTMASTER: Why didn't you? It's a free country, isn't it?

LUTHER: Not yet. I must first strike a blow for freedom and individual liberty and I must found American democracy's principles and the public schools and the Right of Private Interpretation. Then we can do what we want. No, really, I think I could have gotten away with it. But you know that tough old Irish janitor they have over at the Castle Church . . .

(Fade Out)

6 Free Advertising

Catchwords
and Catchpictures

People—particularly women—who patronize public transportation systems these days are in danger of being bewitched by an advertisement picturing a tonsured, Gregory Peckish monk with hypnotic eyes, a Mona Lisa smile, and hands devoutly folded over a loaf of bread. Boasts the blurb at the bottom of this imposing bit of ecclesiastical beefcake: "Out of a tranquil monastery comes the most deeply satisfying bread you have ever tasted." I'll wager that things would become a mite less tranquil in that monastery if some of its denizens could see this Madison Avenue monk. Some of them might even muster a compunction or two about having licensed their "special recipe" for commercial purposes. On the other hand they might defend the deal on the ground that it proves that monasticism really isn't escapist after all.

The power of hidden persuasion being what it is, one wouldn't have too much trouble regarding this bread, subliminally at least, as holy whole wheat, as modern-style manna. Indeed, the aura of sanction and sanctity which the beautiful, if not beatific, monk lends to the loaf almost seems intended to beguile the consumer into thinking that perhaps, after all, he *can* live by bread alone—if it's the *right* bread, the "most deeply satisfying" bread. It's somehow inappropriate that this brand, too, must have a preservative added; alack and alas, it's less than miraculous.

I must admit that the bread in question is pretty good, as present-day prefabricated, chemically concocted breads go (most of them should go and never come back). Nevertheless, soon

63

after my first encounter with the poster's impostor monk I
found myself thinking that maybe I should launch a crusade
under the banner, "Protestants and Other Subversives United
for Separation of Church and Advertising."

A rival baking concern has also been exploiting the religion
gimmick, but this one makes with the humble bit; it actually
admits that man cannot live by bread alone, and every Christmas since 1954 it has ostentatiously said so in big letters on out-
door billboards. Sure to make its way into every sentimental
heart, the poster, in addition to quoting Matt. 4:4, features a
cherubic, golden-haired darling with bowed head and clasped
hands. Less sectarian than the monk poster, it has, according to
its promoters, "compiled an unusual record of market recognition from the press, the clergy and spiritual leaders of many
faiths" and "has often been used as the object of holiday sermons." In fact, the demand for prints of the poster has become
so great in this most religious and most secular of lands that its
sponsor has prepared for distribution 19-in. by 11-in. prints in
full color, suitable for framing and "available to church, Sunday and Temple school teachers for hanging on classroom
walls." A minister's sermonette circulated by the sponsoring
baker maintains that the little girl in the picture desires "eleva-
tion of the heart," and rhapsodizes that "her spirit joins with
the praises of the magnificat." (Precocious tyke. And all the
time I thought the wee lass was only make-believe.)

Hmmm. I can see now that POSU's struggle is going to be
uphill. As Robert Louis Stevenson once wrote, "Man is a crea-
ture who lives not by bread alone, but principally by catch-
words." And catchpictures.

Rush Coupon
Now!

You, dear reader, know us as crusaders. One of our crusades is
against commercialism; we do not think everyone ought to pay

for every advertisement he sees. (We don't get along too well with our own advertising department.) So we here reproduce, free of charge and as a public service, a number of advertisements we have seen lately.

The A.F.C. Fire Equipment Service, Inc., Irvington, New Jersey, advertises itself as "the first Christ-centered fire extinguisher sales and service corporation in the United States." The company's letterhead, by the way, uses a Star of David as an emblem, and the text, "I must be about my Father's business," as a slogan.

"Prepare now for the inevitable," advises the Pet Memorial Products Co., Hutchinson, Kansas. How? By sending $12.95 for a waterproof, rodentproof, machine-press-contoured, satin-padded, exterior wrought-iron black, gold-mist finished burial vault for your small pet. What if our pet is—or was—a rodent?

The Airlines Clergy Bureau, Sacramento, California, announces that it is working on a 50 per cent courtesy discount on clergy airline fares. Reporting its success in getting a few domestic airlines to grant the reduction ("we stand on the threshold"), the bureau rejoices, "Now thanks be unto God, which always causeth us to triumph . . ." (II Cor. 2:14). Fly now, pray later?

If you want to order the book, *Be a Terrifying DESTRUCTIVE Self-Defense Fighter in Just 30 Days,* from its author, Joe Weider, Union City, New Jersey ("centuries-old methods of combat taken from the archives of the . . . killer cult temples . . . Nazi and Communist Secret Police . . . with one chop . . . reduce hoodlums and wise guys into yellow-belly cowards and make them writhe in pain—as if they were mere children!"), you have to sign a coupon which advises the moral Mr. Weider, "Yes, Joe, I need the secret, hidden destructive powers you will reveal. I need them as an effective weapon to overcome any aggressive attackers who threaten me. I enclose 25 cents . . ."

Write Box 139, the *National Review,* if you can answer this Personal Advertisement: "Will any Protestant minister in the midtown Manhattan area who reads *National Review* please send name of his church to displaced conservative?"

Telit Industries, Chicago, offers preachers a portable sermon prompter called TelExecutive. "Eliminate any chance of stage fright, speech stumbling, speech memorizing." Price $169.50.

Gaylords on the Hill, a restaurant in Boulder, Colorado, sells "The Sexburger," which it proudly says is "the University Sanctioned Overnight Sandwich." In London, Trappist monks of the Caldey Island abbey have opened a perfume shop—an outlet for their $28,000-a-year cologne-making industry. If you visit the shop, don't carry in any smelly Trappist cheese.

Argosy Book Stores, New York City, offers (for only $15.00) a "Broadside Playbill," 1869 vintage, advertising a "Wonderful Two-Headed Girl . . . with Two Separate, Well Developed Heads and Two Separate and Distinct Sets of Arms and Shoulders . . . no monstrosity . . ."

And from Christian Supply, Baldwin Park, California, you can get for a buck each, such bargain books as *Faith Made Easy, Soul-Winning Made Easy,* and *Soul-Building Made Easy,* and, for $1.25, *Divorce Problem Made Easy*—this last "a fascinating liberal approach from a conservative Biblical point of view."

Slenderella

I PRAYED MYSELF SLIM. By Deborah Pierce as told to Frances Spatz Leighton. Citadel, $2.95.

This one is enough to make even Norman Vincent Peale wince. (At least its author had the graciousness not to title it *The Power of Positive Shrinking.*) Harry Emerson Fosdick, among others, has had some rather withering words for people who in their prayers regard God as if he were an all-purpose whimpleaser, a sort of cosmic bellhop. But Deborah Pierce's God wouldn't settle for mere bellhopping, mind you; he had a much higher ambition: to become a professional slenderizer. And apparently he made the grade.

As a chubby-cheeked, calorie-collecting coed, Debbie was avoided by men, gossiped about by girls. Then one day disconsolate Debbie suddenly experienced "a strange exultant feeling"—as if "on the verge of a miracle"; lo and behold, she had been visited by the recollection (a real epiphany, it would seem) that *gluttony is one of the seven deadly sins*. From there on it was just a matter of melba toast, celery stalks, and water cress—plus daily appeals to the "Greatest Power" to pull her out of "the dark and lonely abyss of gluttony." Having (1) galvanized her gumption; and (2) gotten God on her side, she carried through on a crash diet and in ten months' time was eighty-two pounds lighter and having dates, dates, dates (she even got to go to the governor's inaugural ball). No longer a waddling wallflower, thanks be to God!

Eventually, Debbie got her just deserts for giving up a life of just desserts: she made her way—with God's help, of course—in the worlds of television, beauty contests, and high-fashion modeling. She assures us, however, that despite the fact that fame befell her, she has remained humble: "I started to worry that all this concentration on beauty and self-exhibition for applause might go to my head, but I was saved from conceit by Love." Early this year Debbie married her Love, who—and we dimly perceive an irony here—is an army instructor in solid fuels.

Deborah's dieting suggestions, if unoriginal, at least have the virtue of being commonsensical—except for the use of a verse from the New Testament as a kind of magical incantation. The bulk of the book is devoted to menus and prayers. We're no judge of diets, but the lunch for the regimen's first week looks awfully grim: "Sip two glasses of water and nibble carrot and celery stalks while reading something which will hold your attention" (the latter instruction is no doubt intended as a means of distracting the dieter from the growls of protesting innards). As for the lady's prayers, we dislike judging anyone's —and we don't doubt the sincerity of hers. But most readers are likely to be either embarrassed or amused—or both—when a good appetite is made to seem the worst of sins (for example: "Mine is a broken and contrite heart, O Lord, for I yielded today to the temptation of a rich dessert, and afterwards the guilt of my sin hung heavy upon my heart . . ."). Only three or four of the fifty-eight prayers acknowledge the existence of other people.

The reviewer, a Jack Spratt type who hardly casts a decent shadow, admittedly has difficulty empathizing with Debbie. But so would a good many fat people. For one thing, she maintains that excess avoirdupois is simply a matter of overeating and that "what I have done can be done by anyone with faith." What about the unfortunate souls who are overweight because of a glandular malady? Moreover, she contends that nobody respects a fat person. Well, we can think of *several* fat people who merit respect. (We suspect that what she really means is that fat people don't have much sex appeal.) In her foreword Debbie eschews sectarian prejudice and prays that "we will all end up together in Heaven." We hope so too. But we're just mean enough to hope that her celestial subdivision has its full quota—nay, an overfilled quota—of five-by-five heavenly heavies.

It's easy enough to chide the Deborah Pierces who eagerly but unwittingly make fools of themselves in print. The real indictment is the fact that the kind of popular piety Deborah Pierce represents is all too typical—a bandwagon we all too often scramble breathlessly aboard.

The Great Imperative

Down in Knoxville, Tennessee, there's a school called Cooper Institute, Inc. Its letterhead heralds it as "The School That's Different." And that it is.

Of late, Cooper Institute has been busy launching a course in medical insurance. The "insurance age" in medicine has come upon us so fast, maintains the Institute, that "there is a very real danger that the numerous voluntary health and medical insurance plans, seen by the medical profession itself as the last hope of avoiding socialized medicine, may bog down and fail for lack of trained personnel, thereby throwing our civilization, as it were, into socialism by default." To head its new program, the Institute has engaged Mr. Walter L. Williams, a "lifelong" medical insurance adjuster. Featured in the promotion material is a nine-page, single-spaced letter from Mr. Williams. It, too, is different. Astounding, in fact.

Heretofore we had thought of insurance simply as a social device enabling individuals to reduce or eliminate certain measurable risks of economic loss by means of a system of equitable contributions. But insurance is a great deal more than that, Mr. Williams informs us. Not only is it "the essential undergirding of our free enterprise system" and "our ultimate defense weapon against communism"; it is—so Williams' letter tells us no less than fourteen times—"co-conservator with the churches of the moral heritage of Western Civilization." Moreover, Christianity cannot exist in today's world without the help of insurance:

> You could have Christianity in its sense of personal responsibility without insurance as in the primitive societies; . . . you can have mechanization without insurance as in the communistic societies today; but . . . you cannot have Christianity (moral responsibility) plus mechanization without insurance. . . . Insurance is the means by which the natural and divine law flows into the practical affairs of men after mechanization.

Further along, Mr. Williams deals with the "rule on moral hazard" and God's role in the insurance business:

> Moral hazard (departures from normal moral behavior as understood in the framework of our religious heritage) is the one hazard that cannot be insured. . . . A thing does not have to be illegal to be uninsurable. For example, the moral transgression of gluttony is beyond the reach of the Supreme Court, but it is not beyond the reach of an insurance underwriter . . . for in the final analysis the actuarial tables, insofar as the crime, greed and stupidity of man can be removed from them, must be writ by the hand of God, according to the immutable laws of the universe.

Williams concludes with a plea to the churches to support his course. Why "come before the churches in this perhaps unprecedented way"? "We do this at a critical hour in the history of our free enterprise system. . . . Freedom of worship and freedom of enterprise are inseparably bound together."

> We do it with a sense of mission, lest some future Toynbee come to poke about in the ruins of Western Civilization, flicking a lizard here, an anthill there, have warranty to say, "Curious, that a civilization founded on a tradition of moral responsibility could not understand and appreciate that the coming of mechanization made a workable insurance system oriented to moral responsibility the great imperative."

How very reassuring to know just what the great imperative is, and especially to know that "our insurance system is clearly an outgrowth of Biblical law." Up to now we had always been a bit uneasy about having even a small amount of insurance; we kept thinking about the Sermon on the Mount, particularly the verse that says, "Take therefore no thought for the morrow: for the morrow shall take thought for the things of itself." But it's all quite clear now. Mechanization, Mr. Williams would no doubt assure us, has made obsolete that small section of the Bible and what it says about moral responsibility—anyway, the churches and the insurance companies have plenty to co-conserve as it is.

Still, we can't help feeling that the Bible won't be quite the same without the Sermon on the Mount. And then there's that passage in Hebrews which describes Christians as strangers and exiles on the earth . . .

Addenda to a College Catalogue

Autumn, 1962. Courses accredited by Southern College Association.

Notice: The following courses have been dropped:

Music 564: Accidentals and Chromatics. Future music courses will introduce students only to white keys.

Ag 404: Morphology of Hybrids. Biological and botanical miscegenation. Students interested in this matter are invited to transfer to midwest corn-belt universities.

Art 441: Southern Regional Folk Architecture. Field trips to primitive Georgia Negro churches canceled. Churches have been burned.

Rel 301: Introduction to Sin. This course has been changed to *Hubris 301.* Field trips transferred from Bourbon Street, New Orleans, to northern white Protestant suburban churches.

The following courses have been added:

Pol Sc 308: Theory and Practice of Insurrection. Historical guide to Whisky Rebellion, July 26 revolution, and other non-Gandhian political realignments. Prerequisite: consent of instructor. Course limited to 3,000 students. Sun 8:00. Inst: *E. Walker.*

Pol Sc 309: Advanced Constitutional Theory. The Doctrine of Interposition in American history. Introduction to writings of John C. Calhoun. All texts dated pre-1861. Sun 8:00. Inst: *R. Barnett.*

Econ 404: Disintegration of Systems. Formerly called Integration of Systems. Mon 9:00.

Am Hist 419: General Introduction to American History. Comprehensive coverage of entire national period, 1776–1861 and 1865–1962. Misses no details. Tues 10:00.

Charm 100: Introduction to Etiquette. Beauty, charm, poise, restraint, ballet, and etiquette. Designed to keep alive the southern traditions of graciousness and hospitality. Sun 8:00. Inst: *former Miss Americas.*

Ethics 212: Practical Living. Fraternity men only. Note: no coke bottles, zip guns, or razors may be brought to class. Sun 8:00.

Chem 211: Introduction to Incendiaries and Explosives. A

practical course with in-service and on-campus training opportunities. Sun 8:00. Inst: *Tony "Coke Bottle" Cocaciola.*

Ind Arts 109: Industrial and Campus Maintenance. Introductory course in window repair, effigy-removal, statue-defense, policing of grounds, garbage and burned-auto removal. Mon 8:00. Meets at Lyceum.

Mort Sc 402: Introduction to Funerary Arts. Mon 8:00.

Eng 400: Semantics III. Advanced course in semantics, graduate students only. Fall project: Emphasis on practice in translation of "Ah hate nigras" into such terms as "judicial restraint," "southern tradition," "interposition," "this sovereign state." Sun 8:00. Inst: *P. Johnson.*

Rel 204: Bible Translation and Revision. Introduction to text, canon, textual and higher criticism, revision, transmission, translation. Considers interpolations in Northern Standard Revised Version of the Bible, theoretical basis for excision of Acts 17:26, Gal. 3:28, John 3:16.

Godly
Gimmicks

Maybe the approach of Christmas inspires it; at any rate, oozing good will, we offer herewith some free advertising. First, so that Sunday schools can start lining up ticket sales, we call attention to the next offering in the ongoing glut of religious movie spectaculars. A two-page advertisement in *The New York Times* heralds its advent: "One full year before the release of this motion picture, the world is being told that in magnitude, in production, in dramatic splendor . . . it will be the undisputed leader in screen entertainment for 1962." Title of the edifying tidbit: *The Last Days of Sodom and Gomorrah.* Verses 23 and 24 from Genesis 19 are quoted in the ad, thus rendering the film acceptable to all Bible believers.

In case you are wearying of the Lord's Prayer, you might have a go at an alternative invented by a grand old man, O. D. Foster, of the State University of Iowa. Dr. Foster endeavored to pack into a single sentence a philosophy of science and religion which could be repeated "as readily as the Lord's Prayer":

> SPIRITUAL COSMIC CHALLENGE: The more courageously TRUTH is objectively sought and understandingly taught by the honest religionist the more probably will he presage intuitive inspiration toward experiencing extension of participating environmental oneness in SUPREME COSMIC BEING and all Divine inanimate, animate, spiritual concerns through successive advolutions toward evermore enticingly advancing goals.

The other day the H. Fendrich Company of Evansville, Indiana, sent us a letter which began, "Reverend and Dear Sir." Inspired by this salutation we read on, only to note that Fendrich has for some years been offering only to clergymen "reconditioned and repacked cigars" at half price. We were a bit disturbed to note that the company also sells cigars it describes as "off color." Well, well!

The Rev. James Donovan, O.M.I., of Carthage, Missouri, has lent endorsement to the Better Reading Program, Inc., of Chicago. "Every Roman Catholic Priest has the strict obligation of reciting what he calls his Divine Office every day," and, insists Father Donovan, the better-reading course will save the priest at least thirty-five minutes daily. We wonder how fast he could recite the Spiritual Cosmic Challenge.

Our last free ad is taken from a publicity release quoting the evangelist Billy Graham as it prepared us for the appearance of N.B.C.'s TV show, "The World of Billy Graham." You have no idea how hard it is to suppress comment:

> I've been asked many times why these great crowds of people come to these meetings. I don't know the total answer. But I remember Mr. Kennedy, when I was playing golf with him, the President asked me why these people came. He said you could put a politician in Madison Square Garden and he might fill it one or two nights, but he couldn't fill it for 16 weeks.
>
> And I remember when we were in Australia that Sammy Davis, Jr., called me up and he said, "Man," he said, "where do you get

all these people?" He said, "Come on up here to Brisbane and join
me." He said, "Man, you must have something." And I told him,
laughingly, I said, "Well, Sammy, if you were preaching the same
message I was preaching, maybe the people would come." And he
laughed.

The Christmas
Bazaar

"How to Make a Success of Your Church Fair" was the lead
article in a September issue of *Woman's Day,* a monthly read
religiously by the supermarket shoppers of America. It's an
impressive article, especially in regard to what it says about
the Christmas bazaar in an affluent society: "It can be a profitable venture. Proceeds can build a new wing for the church
school [we hope], paint and refurbish a beloved but shabby
interior, landscape and plant the grounds for future garden
parties and receptions, buy a new organ or a set of carillon
bells [again, we hope]." Of course, *Woman's Day* points out,
the Christmas bazaar ought to be practically a year-round
activity. Work on it should start the February before if it is to
be a real success. But in case your churchwomen's group hasn't
been so forehanded and, with Advent almost upon us, is about
to panic, we shall offer some last-minute suggestions.

First, however, let us say that Protestants in particular should
go in for Christmas bazaars. They are tax-free and so win the
good will of shoppers (though not of competitive restaurants
and stores). Being highly commercial ventures, they should be
timed to take place a week or so *before* the minister starts
preaching against highly commercial ventures at Christmas.
There is room for sneaking in many activities not usually con-
doned (St. Luke's Chapel in New York, *Woman's Day* reports,
features fortune tellers and penny pitching for the kiddies).
And, as Professor Gibson Winter points out, the furious activity of bazaars is a creative substitute for the penance system

which Protestantism rejects. So, again, we are all for these enterprises.

Now here are some concrete suggestions for the booths:

Sell copies of Richard Nixon's *My Six Crises* at 10 cents each.

Offer an Irish Linen Eye Chart with Hebrew lettering (available from Serendipity 3, of New York City).

Have a few weighty books for sale—for example, Shorewood Press's *Great Drawings of All Time,* a four-volume set, boxed, $160, weight 36 pounds; or Harcourt, Brace & World's *The Magnificence of Rome,* $200, weight 10 pounds. If you offer books like these, you can make some money on the side and add to the general gaiety of the occasion with a weight-lifting contest.

Sell toy trucks to carry these books around in.

A St. Christopher Key-Chain containing water from the River Jordan would be a good item. Air-mailed to you direct from the Holy Land, through Global Sales Service of San Diego.

Prayer is a nice custom. Foster it and make money by offering sets of 24 cards with "old favorite" graces at mealtime printed on them. Obtainable from Gymcrack, of Wellsville, New York. The cards, as Gymcrack reminds us, "make the custom of grace at mealtime a pleasant and convenient experience for young and old." So there need be no more agony at the table or in the garden.

A very cute item comes from Admark Associates, enterprising Chicago firm—a "unique, flickering, battery-powered candle" that "blinks, twinkles, and winks as the candle sways" (we presume, as the choir member who holds it sways). Good for concerts after office parties.

Since there are likely to be a few sourheads even at a church Christmas bazaar, have London's Shaw Society offer a few anti-Christmas items for sale. We suggest cards (order from the Shaw Society) with a drawing of G. B. Shaw in Santa Claus suit and this quotation: "Courage, friend. We all loathe Christmas, but it comes only once a year and is soon over."

Or, if after all your church desires not to have a Christmas bazaar, a last suggestion: Observe the penitential season of Advent.

Opinion Journals
Anonymous

Six American journals seem to be regarded by the public as in the same league: *America* and *The Commonweal* (Catholic); *The Christian Century* (Protestant); the *Nation* and the *New Republic* (liberal); the *National Review* (conservative). They all sell opinions, often controversial opinions. A mass culture trains people to have homogenized, safe, noncontroversial opinions, and sometimes a mass-minded reader, faced with an article or editorial in one of the six, gets mad and cancels his subscription. Controversial stance or not, opinion journals want to keep their readers. And so that they won't lose the price of a subscription, we have devised a plan providing a replacement for every cancellation. Under this plan, a person who gets provoked at one of the six and cancels his subscription will promptly subscribe to one of the other five. He will then join in forming a club with five people, each mad at a different one of the *other* five journals—so each can continue to read the magazine he has dropped.

Though we can—with difficulty—picture a person getting along without one of the six journals, we believe that a subscriber angry enough to cancel is one who cares—and is likely to be highly curious about what appears in future issues. At regular meetings of the club, he can read his old magazine friend; he can stay mad at the editor—he has made his point— but not miss a thing. For such cancelers, here is a compendium of complaints to be pieced together according to need. Like most of their kind they are abrupt, include a spelling error, deny the editor a second chance:

Item 1 (for all six): Dear Editor. *Item 2 (for all six)*: I have been a faithful reader of your magazine for *x* years. Please cancel my subscription. (*Note: always make* x *a high number.*)

Item 3 (*for* America *and* Commonweal, *Reader Type A*): You Cathlicks are trying to take over America. Why don't you go back home? We belong here. My great-grandfather was a Scot and my great-grandmother an Iroquois. I may be illegitimate, but I *am* a *real* American. *Item 3* (*for* America *and* Commonweal, *Reader Type B*): What kind of Cathlicks are you? I am a real Cathlick, and I'm going back to *Our Sunday Visitor* and the Birch books.

Item 3 (*for* Century, *Reader Type A*): You are soft on Cathlicks. Why don't you tell how the pope is going to take over the White House when the Italian communists take over Rome? *Item 3* (*for* Century, *Reader Type B*): You are too anti-Cathlick. You should be called the *Un*-Christian Century. Ha! Ha!

Item 3 (*for* Nation *and* New Republic, *Reader Type A*): You are socialists in disgise; you are leading us down the road to communism. *Item 3* (*for* Nation *and* New Republic, *Reader Type B*): I used to like you in the 1930's. Now you act as if the Refolution didn't happen.

Item 3 (*for* National Review, *Reader Type A*): You are just a Cathlick magazine in disguise. Your attack on the papal encyclical was just a cover-up to throw us off. *Item 3* (*for* National Review, *Reader Type B*): Why did you repudiate the John Birch Society? What kind of a Cathlick are you?

Item 4 (*for all six*): I never want to see your magazine again. Just for spite, I am going to join a club in which I can read all your competitors.

These samples are free of charge to any Opinion Journals Anonymous club-members-to-be. When is the next meeting?

Trilogy of
Corruptions

MODERN KING JAMES VERSION OF THE HOLY BIBLE, and THE
TEEN-AGE VERSION OF THE HOLY BIBLE. McGraw-Hill,
$7.95 each.

Few publishers have provided us with as fine Bible helps in recent years as has McGraw-Hill; so it is with regret that we announce that the firm has really failed us with its trilogy of
corruptions of the King James Bible (besides the two listed
above there is a children's version, which we are too embarrassed to look into). All three of these versions, the publisher
informs us, are the work of a midwestern bookseller, Jay Green,
Sr., who is credited with taking out all the difficult words but
keeping the *real* Bible—that is, the King James Version—otherwise intact. The books, by the way, have lurid illustrations of
Adam, Abraham, Isaac, Jacob, a priest, a king; three appear in
each, before page 17, at which point, evidently, the illustration
budget ran out. The typography and binding are appropriately
ugly. Mr. Green's versions are designed for Bible readers "who
want God's word in the King James Version with a minimum
of necessary word changes for easier, quicker reading."

Mr. Green undercuts the one feature of the K.J.V. that makes
it worth keeping around: the archaic beauty of its language. He
drops such choice words as wist, discomfit, betimes, assuage,
choler, holpen, emerods, leasing, ouches, clout, trow, besom,
amerce, bruit, champaign, fray, neesing, and bestead. However,
our mighty linguist has deigned to retain assarion, buckler,
mattock, spelt, tabrets, gerah and other highly flavored words
which, it would appear, are in daily use among moderns (teen-
agers or adults). In both volumes he provides a guide to thirty-
nine key categories of the Bible (adultery, chastity, divorce,
drinking, joking, lust, pleasure-seeking, popularity, vanity,
vulgar language, kissing, petting—for these last two he directs

readers to Prov. 20, 21; 6:27–29; 9:17, 18; Jas. 1:13–15) and a handy glossary (fury is pronounced fe-oor-e; eunuch, you-nuck: "a man who has had those parts which make him able to father children cut off or out"). He misdefines unbelief, in his self-chosen "conservative and evangelical" terms, as "not believing what is said, written or taught." He engages in cultural defense: "The KJV is the very matrix from which has come a civilization blessed with more abundance . . ."

In his own prefaces, while protesting against archaisms and "difficult" words, Green uses, or quotes favorably, "whilst" and "prebendary." He asserts that recent translations "carnalize" the Bible with expressions such as "take a chance" and "stomach it," yet he refers to teen-agers (a term itself a carnalization, we'd say) as "kids." The classic format of the Bible he calls "paragraph-per-verse," a phrase that bothers us. Now, we, too, are interested in clarity in Bible translations and would ordinarily join hands with the Mr. Greens of this world. We are particularly impressed by the formidable list of his associates in the teen-age version (Boy Scouts, Young Life, Campus Crusade, Youth for Christ, Public and Private Schools—and Jay Green, Jr.). But Mr. Green's introduction is distorted, and strikes us as dishonest.

In his eagerness to sell his King James Version he accuses all modern translators, especially those of the N.E.B. and R.S.V., of perversions of the text—charges which the lay reader may not always understand. He represents them as conspirators, eager to kill off the K.J.V. (which "impudently refuses to die"); of trying to seduce younger generations from the K.J.V. to their own unsafe Bibles; of "assuming license to correct even the original ancient languages"; of changing doctrines in Isa. 7:14; Matt. 1:25; Rom. 1:17; II Tim. 3:16, and elsewhere; of adding "thousands upon thousands of words" to the Bible. These are all the familiar strictures against the R.S.V., criticisms which responsible conservative evangelicals have long left behind. Green must know better. He must know the rudiments of the textual criticism which he misrepresents. He says of his market: "Teen-agers are smart. They quickly suspect. . . . They want to know if anyone has monkeyed [with the Scripture]." If they are smart, they will discomfit their Bible's editor and in the fray will verbally clout him in the besom until it ouches and he is bruited and bestead. There is a word for this version; it is the first one in Green's glossary: *abomination*.

7 A Chronicle: The Shape of the Week

Missing Persons

Missing persons dominated the news. For instance, Russia's Joseph (Vissarionovich Dzhugashvili) Stalin. Though venerated immediately after his death, he has been downgraded by his successor twice-removed. Missing from his place of honor beside Nikolai Lenin, he now lies in downgraded repose outside the Kremlin wall. Missing persons would be the only loss in a world in which the neutron bomb, now being discussed by Russia and the United States, would be unleashed. We take no small comfort in the knowledge that this neutron bomb would be non-destructive of "things"—it would only destroy persons. Are there better parables for postmodernity?

Missing persons abound in Vol. 1, No. 1, of the *Post Rapture Journal,* a millenarian newspaper selling for five cents and published by John A. Leland, Atlanta, Georgia. The sheet takes literally the various biblical references to people being suddenly and decisively removed from this planet for their Christian faithfulness. Evangelist Leland's paper offers photos of numbers of non-Christians supposedly mourning the departures of Christian relatives and friends. The photos show empty autos, planes, beds, jails—the people having disappeared. Nothing new in that. However, we note one peculiar twist: all Leland's heaven-bound people leave their clothes behind.

Christian stewards will be missing if the American Institute of Motivation Research of Los Angeles, California, has its way. Like the neutron-bomb makers, the institute cares not about persons so much as things—not about people but about their motivations and their money. The institute has been bombarding the clergy with promotion material about its three-year study of factors that motivate people to give tens of thousands of dollars more. Offering help to "you pastors and your clerical assistants [who] have to get by on sub-normal salaries," the institute promises that "your congregation will accept your appeals for what they really are: *the appeals of God.*" So perhaps the institute does care for at least *some* persons—clergymen. It even advertises literature giving advice to clergymen on "how to avoid, and how to survive, heart attack, cerebral hemorrhage and atherosclerosis." (These three diseases kill and cripple more clergymen than do others, thus "causing more disruptions in church efficiency.")

We'd like to see persons missing from the cover of the *Watchman-Examiner.* Evidently from time immemorial, every issue of this "National Baptist Journal" has carried a portrait of a Baptist clergyman. These are good men and faithful servants, often handsome and almost always pleasant-looking. But is this what Protestantism wants most of all to stress? It has always seemed curious to us that a magazine published by a group highly critical of Catholic clericalism should each week adorn its front cover with a picture of a cleric. We move that those who watch the *Watchman* make suggestions to its editors on what to put on the cover and how to relegate the clergy portraits to the Bureau of Missing Parsons.

Sick
Jokes

Sick jokes seemed to dominate the week. Take, for instance, the headliner hurricane posing behind the soft and gentle name, "Carla." Take—yes, *you* take—scientist Edward Teller's assurance that 90 per cent of our nation's citizens would survive an H-bomb war, that in three to four years the country could be rebuilt, that "only" twenty million Americans would lose their lives in such a war. And then there was the sickness of a comedian named Paar, filming television shows at the border Where They Could Start to End Everything, offering banal and uninformed comment on world affairs.

Everywhere we turned this week the sickness seemed to have spread. The Israeli Government Tourist Corporation had to release one of its women guides for making "jokes in bad taste" while conducting tours of holy places. And from a visitor to Japan came word that next to the Hiroshima peace memorial a huckster sells replicas of the United States A-bomb plane.

For many years Miss Mary Spencer of Elizaville, Kentucky, has been playing a religious joke on her sister, Miss Ollie, who is treasurer, trustee, steward, custodian, and the entire congregation of Clover Hill Methodist Church, where the Rev. Harry Oldaker is pastor. If sister Mary would join, the congregation would grow by 100 per cent (and what would *Together* magazine do with *that* statistic?). But no. According to the press release, Miss Mary "doesn't attend and never has belonged to a church." In the First Baptist Church at Mar Vista, California, the John H. Chapman family sings the hymns and reads the Scriptures so loudly during services that the minister has had to get a court injunction to bar them from attending the church. The joke they were playing was occasioned by the fact that they had been excommunicated.

On the High Church High Jinks front: In a *Living Church* magazine poll seeking suggestions for a new name for the Protestant Episcopal Church, one person came up with "Pecusalite"; another, "the Church of England in the Colonies." And along with these individual eccentricities, *one hundred* respondents offered *"The* Holy Catholic Church." (There *were* some sensible proposals, though.)

Suggested autumn reading: *Magnetohydrodynamics: Proceedings of the Fourth Biennial Gas Dynamics Symposium* (Northwestern University Press). Northwestern is in Illinois;

could that state's rhetorical Senator Everett M. Dirksen by any chance have been keynoter at the symposium?

The advertisement of the Sick Joke Week: Note-Lok Enterprises, Cambridge City, Indiana, offers for $3.95 what is surely an immoral device for preachers of morality. Exhorts the blurb: "Stop being obvious. . . . You can have copious notes, even a short sermon, bound right into your Bible each Sunday. *And,* you can be sure your audience will not see . . ."

Outlived Usefulness

Thoughts about people who have outlived their usefulness kept bobbing up this week. Take St. Philomena. When we opened a bill from the St. Benet bookstore in Chicago the other day, out dropped a Philomena saint's card. St. Benet makes it a practice to send along with monthly bills an occasional bookmark or prayer card. Now that Philomena has been decanonized by Pope John XXIII because her existence is doubted, her saint's cards are apparently in oversupply.

An English butcher has passed his time of usefulness. Until recently a disconcerting official notice on the penny-a-turn turnstiles at the entrances to public lavatories in Ashbourne, Derbyshire, advised: "If unable to operate the turnstile, please contact butcher at adjoining premises." Now the government, responding to protests from women who got stuck in the "gorilla cages"—as a woman M.P. termed them—has ordered the offending obstacles removed from all public lavatories.

Others who have outlived their usefulness? Well, how about General Edwin A. Walker, who plans to dedicate his life to a Birch-type mission? Or the Conformist—in the light of this Greenwich Village sign: "Nonconformity taught here." Or the corporeal nature of N. Khrushchev, in the light of Major Gherman Titov's comment: "We're very proud Premier Khrushchev called Gagarin and me heavenly brothers. I must let you in on a secret. We cosmonauts and many Soviet people call Khrushchev our heavenly Father."

Some people just can't outlive their usefulness to the church. Thus a Methodist district superintendent in Iowa issued this ukase in his newsletter calling for attendance at a subdistrict meeting: "No minister is excused except for illness or death . . . such excuses must be O.K.d by the D.S." St. Peter at the gate upstaged by an Iowa Methodist district superintendent!

The hoary head and the wisdom of age are despised and outlived by the cult of youth in this week's theological blurb from MGM, the *King of Kings* remaker. Writes Director Nicholas Ray: "Essentially, the story of Jesus and the people of his age is a story about, and for, young people. We wanted that quality of youth . . ." That, Mr. Ray, is blasphemy. And on the fact that six different nationalities and four different languages are represented in the *Kings* cast of disciples, Royal Dano, the oldest young disciple, comments: "This is faithful to the New Testament." Evidently non-Hollywood biblical scholars have outlived their usefulness, too.

Double
Exposures

Russian propagandists recently used an old photo of Japanese soldiers burning a Chinese village; only this time they said it was Germans burning a Russian village. Double exposure: first for Chinese propaganda, then for anti-NATO use. Now they've acknowledged their mistake—but was it a mistake or an attempt at deception? There were other double exposures to shape the week. Stanley Fuller-Wall was exposed to doubled crises when his two wives, one aged 82, the other 44, died the same day in London. The bigamist attended the funeral of the older and richer one. The *nee*-Bouviers were doubly exposed to the fashion world, as Mrs. Kennedy and her sister Princess Radziwill both made the list of the world's "best-dressed."

But this week's chief double exposure, the one that provides the topic for our sermon, comes from New York. Advertisers like to get double exposures out of the words critics and reviewers write by quoting from favorable notices in their promotion materials—a perfectly legitimate thing to do, so long as the blurb is faithful to the original context. Last week, as everyone must know by now, the Broadway critics were rather hard on a show called *Subways Are for Sleeping.* So stunt-man producer David Merrick looked up in the phone book seven men's names which were identical to those of the critics. He dined the seven men, took them to the play, got rave notices from them, and contrived an advertisement in which he placed their pictures and names beside their enthusiastic comments. One newspaper inadvertently accepted and printed the ad. The Better Business Bureau frowned.

We are interested in a Better Business Bureau to oversee the other practice involved here: taking out of context words from reviews for use in advertisements. Let's play with an illustration. Suppose one of our dauntless, jaundiced, full-of-integrity reviewers discusses Otis Ebis' newest book, *Ivy League for Every Drop of Rain That Falls,* in terms such as these: "Another reviewer who really knows that this is pap insists that it is good—but only because he's engaged to the publisher's daughter. No one else likes it. Indeed, it is astonishing that a creative publisher would touch it. We have our own new theories about how this crassly commercial contribution to positive thinking got printed. It is a potboiler, designed to exploit anxieties. We can hardly describe it; it seems incredible that such drivel can be printed today. We could not put it down because we paged through it at a bus stop and no trash can was handy."

Now, let us look at its double exposure in advertisement, aided by a bit of cropping and dot-dot-dotting:

"THE CHRISTIAN CENTURY" SAYS OF THIS BOOK: ". . . astonishing . . . a creative publisher . . . new theories . . . incredible . . . we can hardly describe it . . . we could not put it down . . ." And then just to make sure, the blurb would add, "The *Century* reviewer says that even his father is enthusiastic

('Pap insists that it is good . . .')" If you look you will find
that all the words are there.

So the reviewer keeps his integrity, the bookseller gets your
money, *The Christian Century* precariously keeps its reputa-
tion. And the publisher gets a double exposure out of the
words.

To
Puff

The Federal Trade Commission's decision to ban "harmless
exaggeration or puffing" from television commercials took
center stage among the week's events. Though other events
made more noise, this one could actually alter our way of life.
What sparked the decision? For a Rapid Shave commercial, the
Colgate-Palmolive Company and its advertising agency had a
sheet of clear plastic sprayed with sand (you could have rubbed
it off with your finger). Then, with cameras grinding away,
"super-moisturized" Rapid Shave was sprayed on the fake sandpaper and—you guessed it—a razor removed the sand as an
announcer solemnly declared that a piece of sandpaper was
being shaved. The FTC said that its agents tried to use Rapid
Shave in shaving real sandpaper of the same grain, and found
that it couldn't be done in sixty seconds—the length of the
commercial—even if the sandpaper had been soaked in Rapid
Shave for an hour. So no more "harmless puffing," says the
FTC. But what will we do without it?

Once a memo from a Hearst editor to his underlings sent a
young evangelist on his way. It took but two words: "Puff
Graham!" The same process goes on today. In Penang, Malaya,
one can pray and thus "Puff Philip Minh." Philip Minh was a
saintly priest who in the nineteenth century was beheaded
during a wave of anti-Catholic persecution in southeast Asia.
A campaign is under way to have him canonized. One trouble:
Malayans have to prove that at least two miracles were worked

through his intercessory activities. The Vatican desires the proof, and Malayans have been asked to pray for that proof. Prayer puffs, we call it.

There are also preaching puffs: Protestants are guilty on this front. Harmless little exaggerations abound whenever a man mounts his tub to raise money for the budget. You know the old stewardship-season chestnut: A man gives money to the church; the more he gives the richer he gets; when asked his money-making methods he asserts, "It's easy. I shovel into God's granary and he shovels into mine. He uses the bigger shovel." FTC, will you be consistent and ban that kind of harmless exaggeration?

"To puff" means to bring the insignificant into significance. We saw a good deal of that in recent weeks as obsolete textbooks and obscene sexbooks were puffed into prominence by groups not usually known for their literacy. We refer to groups like the school board in Wisconsin that promoted McGuffey's readers; and the school out West that unintentionally helped sell Tarzan books as a result of its complaint that Jane became Mrs. Tarzan without benefit of clergy; and the police censors who proved themselves to be avid readers of Henry Miller's *Tropic of Cancer.*

If the *Canadian Churchman* (Anglican) has its way, comfort-minded advertisers will have a hard time in the future. No more rubber-padded kneelers, no more gold curtains in churches, no more excess outside lighting and plush fixtures. Why? The road to heaven is supposed to be rough: "We already have more holy hardware and software than we know what to do with."

Question: Will the deep, deep inhalers in cigarette commercials be forced to refrain from "exaggerated and harmless puffs"?

Singing
the Unsung

This is the time for us to present awards for outstanding achievements during the past year. Most of the people we choose to honor here have gone unnoticed by the Nobel, Pulitzer, Bollingen, and Miss America judges, but all of them have left their mark:

First Award goes to the proofreader or the translator (or perhaps both) of the book *Gherman Titov: First Man to Spend a Day in Space* (Crosscurrents Press). On page 99 Titov reports: "In order to 'quiet' my 'naughty' vestibular system, I cautiously found the most comfortable position in the chair and—fainted. The nausea gradually went down, and things became much better . . ." Inserted into our copy by the publisher was a slip reading: "Erratum: p. 99 line 12 'fainted' should read 'remained still.' " Thus our faith in Soviet semantic expertise (tin-god, clay-feet department) is restored.

Second Award goes to Joseph R. Morse of the Airlines Clergy Bureau of Sacramento, California. Not long ago this column took notice of his efforts to obtain reduced airline fares for clergymen. Now he sends us another report: "To all Ministers: Greetings in the Name of our Lord. I have fought a good fight, I have finished my course, I have kept the faith; henceforth there is laid up for *you* a reduced rate on airlines, hotels, motels, and car rentals." The old Hebrews, we remember, refrained from promiscuous mouthing of the name of the Lord. That was a good idea.

Third Award goes to Elizabeth Bussing for restoring our faith in the soundness of the Episcopal dollar. Soliciting gifts for the Episcopal Church Center in the October, 1962, *Episcopalian,* she suggested, under "more modest opportunities": $8,000 windows and a $10,000 reredos.

Fourth Award goes to the teen-agers in the United Church of Christ for showing wisdom beyond their years. When asked to list "the funniest book I ever read," not far down the list from the leader (*Kids Say the Darndest Things*), they cited Richard Nixon's *Six Crises*.

Fifth Award, distinguishing the most far-sighted church of the year, goes—naturally—to a Southern Baptist congregation, First Baptist Church of Cape Canaveral's neighboring town, Cocoa. "We're concerned," declared the members in a formal memorandum to the Southern Baptist Convention, "that Southern Baptists select, qualify and train men as chaplains to go along on manned space flights." It's not too soon to make sure that the first sky pilots to the space men will be orthodox—though one wonders what Presbyterian Glenn would say about this idea.

Sixth Award, for keeping alive our faith in German thoroughness, goes to the *Evangelisches Verlagswerk* of Stuttgart, publishers of "Pocketbook of the Protestant Church in Germany." Be sure your tailor provides big pockets: the *Taschenbuch* has 900 pages.

Seventh Award, for bestowing the year's greatest gift of happiness on all within earshot, goes to Washington Cathedral, which announces the installation of a ten-bell peal set on which more than 3,600,000 changes can be rung. Says the announcement: "The cascade of notes is often described as invariably joyous, never doleful." There are sermons in that sentence. Ring out the old, ring in the new!

The Boom and
the Whisper

The Supreme Court held by a seven-to-two vote last week that local authorities operating airports must compensate owners of nearby property for losses caused them by the "noise, vibration and fear" produced by low-flying planes. It strikes us as remarkable that in this age of anxiety anyone should get the idea that somebody can compensate us for our fears if we live near enough to the noise that prompts them.

But that aside. As it happens, the Pittsburgh home whose owner set this test case in motion is now functioning as a church—St. Philip's Episcopal. The present users say that "it is a bit noisy at times," but they're "not bothered too much." No doubt they're sincere: churchgoers often become impervious to noise. After all, on ten thousand Sundays they've had shouted at them a "call to worship" that is really designed to beat down the Sunday-school kids: "The Lord is in his holy temple; let all the earth keep silence before him" (Hab. 2:20). Next time you hear a barrel-larynxed cassock-wearer holler that, test it on your decibel-counter. Or try the method of the Rocky Mount Ministers Fellowship, which urges daily ringing of church bells to encourage people to join in *silent* prayer: Make noise to make silence!

The same day that the court ruled on the issue, a B-58 round-tripped America in 4 hours and 42 minutes, leaving a train of broken windows, cracked plaster, and fear. "One woman in Pittsburgh thought her furnace had blown up," *The New York Times* reported solemnly. Who will compensate her for *that* fearful thought? And what is wrong with these Pittsburghers anyhow?

There is no telling how much space the Supreme Court decision is going to cover. We see a number of possible consequences. In Milwaukee one Otto Eberle, who installs and repairs organs, insists that sonic booms are knocking his ten thousand times ten thousands of organ pipes out of pitch. High registers of organs need daily tuning. Will local airports now have to pay the bill? We foresee a new letterhead: "MILWAUKEE AIRCRAFT AUTHORITY ORGAN TUNING DIVISION (Upper Register Echelon)."

What about "fear" caused not by the bang but by the whimper, not by the boom but by the whisper? The world worried about that, too, this week. Senator Kefauver began investigations on the high cost of hearing aids. (In the noisy age we may stop wanting them altogether.) In Des Moines a telephone operator was denied unemployment benefits because of a "bad taste" remark she made "with her key open"—a remark that led to her firing. She overheard a Council Bluffs woman and a Boone man talking and commented, "They are making love." Is the Supreme Court worried about the whisper of fear that must be vibrating in all the telephone operators in Iowa?

Overseas, courts of law haven't yet taken up this problem. Soviet radio stations use whispering sirens (female gender) to cause "noise, vibration, and fear" in Soviet seminarians, to distract them from their theological studies. What court will hear *their* case?

It is every man for himself, after all, against the boom and the whisper. And nine old men can do little to help compensate us for our fears.

8 Desperate Causes

May St. Rita
Help Them!

We like to read in the lives of the saints, and do it almost every day. Lately we have been reading the life of Rita of Cascia, who died in the fifteenth century but was canonized only in 1900. Though Philomena remains the patron saint of this column, we find Rita very attractive, especially since she is the "saint of impossible and desperate causes." We have compiled a little list of impossible and desperate causes to which we wish lots of luck and Rita's assistance:

The Turkish Information Office, New York City, which informs us that a British photographic team headed by Hamish McInnes [*sic*] intends to film a documentary on the authentic ruins of Noah's Ark on Mount Ararat.

The advertiser in the tabloid *Enquirer* who describes himself as "college teacher, Swiss, gentleman, no prejudices whatsoever" and announces that he "seeks lady with pronounced and buxom hips. Primary school education sufficient. True romance. English unnecessary if speaking any Latin language." (But plainly he *does* have a prejudice—against unpronounced, nonbuxom hips.)

The philosophy department at Wheaton College, Wheaton, Illinois, in the preparation for its ninth philosophy conference, subject of which will be "The Philosophy of Herman Dooyeweerd." Conference lecturers are to present papers on "Dooyeweerd's Metaphysics," "Dooyeweerd's Criticism of Classical Philosophy," "Dooyeweerd's Philosophical Method," "Dooyeweerd and His Influence," "Dooyeweerd and Philosophical Objectivity"—and, perhaps most important, "What is Dooye-weerd's Philosophy?"

Safa al-Khulusi, doctor of literature at London University, in his campaign to bring Shakespeare into the Arab camp. The learned doctor claims that an Arab sailor named "Sheikh Zubair" went to England and there came to be known as Shakespeare. (Zubair is a district of Basra, a southern province of Iraq.)

British Methodist Leslie Weatherhead, who wants to expunge from the Bible "a lot of bloody massacres and a lot of smutty little pieces that choir boys read on the quiet."

Here's a desperate cause that strikes us as desperate *in excelsis:* The Rev. Dr. Thomas A. Fry, Jr., of First Presbyterian Church in Dallas, in an effort to combat our increasing and highly unchristian divorce rates, proposes that not only brides and grooms but all attendants at weddings in Christian churches be required to take a vow: "Do you, the wedding party, representing your community and the circle of friends, pledge yourself to those acts and attitudes that will make this marriage grow in its love, permanence and responsibility?" We bet that, after taking the vow, the wedding guests will *still* throw rice, tie old shoes on the happy couple's car, make with charivari and all the rest of the pagan ritual. They'll probably even march in and out to Lohengrin and Mendelssohn. But it's a nice try, Dr. Fry; may St. Rita help you!

We also beseech Rita's help for the good health of the thousands of comb fish from the Sea of Galilee which, through the joint effort of the Israeli fishery department and Twentieth Century Fox, were flown in to Hollywood in the desperate cause of lending realism to the coming film, *The Greatest Story Ever Told,* based on the Oursler story.

By the way, Burgo Partridge's *A History of Orgies,* which our researcher turned up at the Cokesbury bookstore in Chicago, can now be bought at clearance from Publishers Central Bureau, 100 East 29th Street, New York 16. Suppressing it is our own desperate cause.

"To Irma,
Who Will Know Why"

Very likely the people who make Mercedes-Benz automobiles build them only so they can finish off with that awesomely symmetrical trinitarian crest which is their trademark. And no doubt the people who make Pall Mall cigarettes do so just for the sheer delight of seeing the coat of arms stamped on billions of cigarette papers. So, too, there must be authors who see intrinsic worth in the dedication page of a book. For one thing, many readers do not get past the dedication page, which is often much more interesting than the table of contents. It's quite possible, then, that some authors write books just so they can dedicate them.

We regularly watch the *Century*'s shelves of books for review, for trends in dedications. We can report that the cosmic-metaphysical-everything-*and*-the-kitchen-sink kind of dedication which reveals the substance of the book in outline is decreasing in favor, except in works issuing from vanity presses. You know the type: "To Serena, who taught me all that this book knows about essences and the subtle infusions of many kinds of nuances that, as ingredients of life . . ." (This, of course, on the dedication page of a book on the uses of garlic.) In its place a cryptic quality is coming into favor.

Even in dedications redeemed by brevity one finds subtleties revealing a good deal about the authors. Thus in the family-tree type there are several basics. The cocksure author: "To Frieda." The less sure: "To Frieda, to whom I owe everything." The insecure: "To Frieda and her friends." Sometimes the dedication page explains how the author was able to make his way through the valley: "To Frieda, who kept playing Theodore Bikel records and preparing braunschweiger sandwiches so that little Brigitte's crying would not distract me and who . . ." Just once we'd like to see: "To Frieda, who had the courage to complain about the time I took away from family affairs, and who would say, 'You lout, it's about time you went to the laundromat' and who thus benefited humanity by shortening this book." Or better: "To Frieda, who was secretly glad I wrote this book because it kept me out of family circulation."

Then there are the coy ones. Like the S. V. Benéts, who dedicated a co-authored book to their children, their other "joint products." And the teasers. They are the worst; you never get past their dedication pages for wondering. "To Irma, who will know why." Or "To Myrtle, who was there when IT happened."

Just as the vanity press books have the longest, most earnest dedications, so the best-known authors are the least predictable. Billy Graham, for instance, didn't dedicate his newest book to anybody. Fulton J. Sheen, a latter-day *jongleur de Notre Dame,* inscribes *Go to Heaven* to "the LADY who looked down to Heaven as she held Heaven in her arms." We cannot but feel, however, that this reverence is penultimate to the dedication the Reverend George M. Horne, TH.B., LL.B., gives to his new vanity-of-vanities, *The Twentieth Century Cross,* a mongrel of a book against mongrelization, a disintegrative tract against integration: "Segregation is not only sanctioned, but demanded by both Old and New Testaments." To whom could one dedicate such an effort? You guessed it—the ultimate: ". . . but I dedicate these pages to God Almighty, to whom I have long since dedicated my mind, body, and soul without reservations, mental evasions, or equivocations."

Just what God needed.

Speaking of Masquerades . . .

Persons and things are not always what they appear to be. As a service, our detectives have reached into their files of incognitos and cover-ups and brought forth these items as evidence:

In Princeton, New Jersey, three visiting priests were arrested by state troopers. Later Governor Richard Hughes apologized, explaining that a tipster had seen the priests changing from civvies into clerical garb, mistook their sleeveless amice (vests) for shoulder holsters, hoodlum-type. Brethren of the cloth: as you don your cassocks, watch your incognitos!

In Milan, Italy, police arrested four persons whose daytime business—manufacturing souvenir religious medals—was a cover-up for their nighttime occupation: turning out phony money. Our undercover man learned that the moonlighting activity produced "almost perfect" 500-lire pieces; he had no comment on the quality of the medals struck in daylight.

That incognito playwright known as William Shakespeare is being scrutinized anew. Some time ago this column took note of the theory that he was really an Arab named Sheikh Zubair. The conclusion that lines such as, "It is the East, and Juliet is the sun," prove "beyond doubt" that the Bard had Arab blood, has now been challenged by a Texan writing to the *Toledo Blade* to aver that William was really a pre-Texas Texan, an Indian of the Blackfriars tribe, known as Little Running Words of the Brazos. Proof? Well, note the Shakespearean references to horses ("My kingdom . . .") and to open spaces ("My soul hath elbow-room . . ."; "enough, with overmeasure").

Undercover etiquette: A *Manchester Guardian* anecdote recounts how a Lord Quickswood remonstrated with a kinsman thus: "Algernon, why have you grown that beard?" "Well, why not? Our Lord is supposed to have been bearded." "That's no answer. Our Lord was not a gentleman." By Quickswood's standard, indeed not. Thank heavens not!

We didn't recognize our national capital in the Youth for Christ press release that told us: "The staid [?] capital city of Washington, D.C., is bracing for a December invasion of teen-agers . . ." Before we advise and consent to that description, we are going to revisit the city beside the Potomac.

Now for some nonincognitos. Witness the classified advertisement placed by one Lincoln Elliott, Olympia, Washington: " 'SUPREME COURT WAS WRONG. I'M FOR GOD' large 2-inch buttons. 50 cents each. Three for $1.00." And the Protestant Council of New York City has prepared another sixty thousand "I Am a Protestant" cards for 1962–63. They have phosphorescent pink borders and room for an emergency telephone number. But don't tell Dr. Schwarz and his crusaders about the color of those borders! No incognito, either, but an honest-to-goodness name: H. E. Barefoot, a Baptist professor of religion at Jackson, Tennessee. Finally, here's a name that may or may not be intended as incognito: the First Alphabet Church of Cleveland, whose pastor is the father of Joe Shelton, a professional boxer.

Christmas—
Four Cents Worth

The United States Post Office Department, making no bones about its desire to make money, has just issued 500,000,000 Christmas stamps—the largest-ever order for a first printing of a United States stamp. Besides bidding fair to put the Christmas seal people out of business, this stamp represents a new phase in American culture. Postmaster General J. Edward Day has resolved a problem that might have stumped Christians of another stripe: how to make the Christian gospel, folly to the Greeks and scandal to the Jews, palatable to all Americans and commercially profitable. His solution amounts to official recognition of Christmas as a *secular* feast.

The stamp, we are told, was contrived without any particular religious symbols so that no one would be offended. Two candles, a holly wreath, the words "4¢ U.S." and "Christmas 1962" are the only elements of its design. The fact is, of course, that holly *is* a particular religious symbol, which some trace back to Roman saturnalia and others to bloody Teutonic tribal ritual. But let that pass. In the spirit of the "[sh!] mas" season we shall volunteer to Mr. Day some other ways to exploit the religious sentiment of the nation commercially. Here are other holidays that need secular updating:

Easter. The obvious design for an Easter postage stamp would show an egg and a lily. But if the USPO wants to make money, why not auction off the space among hat designers (Lilly Daché, Mr. John, Robert Hall)? The stamp would picture the highest bidder's newest creation.

Epiphany (or Twelfth Night, too). The Wise Men will have to go—not much commercial appeal. Make this the festival of the Three Queens, with postage stamps showing tiaras by Harry Winston, Van Cleef & Arpels, and Tiffany, modeled by three reigning movie queens.

Shrove Tuesday. A picture of the Rat Pack at a Mardi Gras party would appropriately decorate a stamp for this occasion.

Mother's Day. The stamp for this third high holy day in the Protestant liturgical year should suggest interfaith amity. How about a reissue of the Whistler's Mother stamp, with the face of Ethel Kennedy superimposed on Whistler's Mother's body?

Palm Sunday. The outstretched palm of Mr. Day, with a dollar sign on it.

Sexagesima Sunday. This would need no symbolism—only the words "We are all for Sexagesima." For aesthetic reasons the middle syllable of the nine would appear in bold print across the whole stamp.

Passion Week. This stamp should be secularized all the way. Hollywood might have some ideas about how to handle it. The story ought to sell well and so take care of early spring PO deficits.

Holy Innocents. This festival, commemorating the Massacre of the Innocents, December 28, needs rejuvenation in America and could stand some updating. Two stamps would be needed: a northern edition with a picture of Ross Barnett and General Edwin A. Walker goading Ole Miss students into action, and a southern version with Earl Warren coercing little white children into going to kindergarten with Negroes.

Reformation Day. Since we Protestants have been so nice about sharing Mother's Day, the Catholics ought to permit a

Reformation stamp. Of course, we are prepared to make it ecumenical. How about a picture of Cardinal Spellman embracing Stanley Lowell, of Protestants and Other Americans United for Separation of Church and State, as they stand in front of a monolith?

All Saints' Day. A picture of the meditation room at the UN would do; its rich hagiological symbolism could commemorate the whole host of American saints.

The possibilities are virtually unlimited. We've already begun to think about the "-mas" stamp for 1963 (5¢ U.S.). It could have a picture of an office party. Or perhaps a tree (north German pagan symbolism and thus offensive to no one) bedecked with dollar signs. Yes, we'd like that. The PO department, we're sure, would too.

9 The Great Crusade

Pelagius
as Patron

Readers may be somewhat taken aback to find us undertaking a discussion of Sunday church bulletins. This medium of communication is not highly regarded by the power elites; it is not reckoned with on Capitol Hill or in the UN chambers or at Radio City. We have no doubt, however, that vast numbers of people are influenced and informed by it. Archaeologists of the future, scuffling around our civilization's remains, are quite likely to find more copies of church bulletins than of *The New York Times* or *Time* magazine. Bulletins are tucked into purses, bureaus, archives, scrapbooks; industries are built on them; contests determine which is best. Are they not of penultimate importance?

Ostensibly, church bulletins exist to list people for whom masses are being said or from whom smörgåsbord tickets can be purchased. There is one problem, however, which frequently confronts their editors: leftover space. Priests and ministers, who abhor silence, also abhor white space. So bulletins are chock-full of tidbits which usually deny the whole purpose of the Christian endeavor. We commend as patron saint of church bulletins Pelagius, the British monk—and contemporary of Simeon Stylites, by the way—who is responsible for the whole moralistic, busy-busy, activistic enterprise within the Christian tradition.

Scores of bulletins reach our office each week, and we have difficulty choosing the best examples out of a morass of typicality. This week let's look at one from a "First" church in Cisco, Texas ("pioneering since 1880"). Its minister is a college roommate of Senator Tower—a fact serving to heighten our anticipation.

After the usual announcements—hymns, orders of service, the week's calendar—St. Pelagius takes over. First we hear of a "church attendance crusade" (church bulletins always have crusades going); for sixteen Sundays members of First Church will find "present" or "absent" checkmarked after their names on a large chart at the entrance. Next the pastor gives the year's advice. Surprises abound: (1) pray; (2) read the Bible; (3) meditate; (4) worship in church—the suspense is too great!—(5) do something for others; (6) be a witness; (7) support the church; (8) dedicate your life; (9) win another life; (10) look up and lift up. But still there is space to be filled. And here Pelagius really triumphs:

Your Church Garden

First, plant five rows of PEAS. Presence, promptness, preparation, purity, and perseverance.

Next to these plant three rows of SQUASH. Squash gossip, squash criticism, squash indifference.

Then plant four rows of LETTUCE. Let us be faithful in duty, let us be loyal and unselfish, let us be true to our obligations and let us love one another.

No garden is complete, of course, without TURNIPS. Turn up for meetings, turn up with a smile, turn up with new ideas, turn up with determination to make everything count for something good and worth while.

Our abhorrence of white space has prompted us to fill this column. And we are only beginning; we consider this topic of such importance that for the first time we write:

(To be continued)

Anti-Pelagian
Crusade

Last week we launched a crusade against the Pelagianism characteristic of those ubiquitous do-it-yourself journals, the Sunday bulletins printed by churches across the land. You will recall (you *will*, won't you?) that we attacked the moralistic aspect of that particular manifestation of Pelagianism: the fact that in their abhorrence of White Space the ministers who edit the bulletins fill in the gaps with pious platitudes that complicate the preaching of the Good News. This week the crusade rolls on.

Our second lesson derives from a bulletin close at hand. We use it to point out the perils of emulation, the risk the unnoted minister takes when he tries to copy procedures employed by noted preachers of the land. Important ministers often list their week's engagements in their Sunday bulletins. What would happen if that technique were imitated in just any church's Sunday bulletin? Incidentally, the technique itself calls for considerable cogitation: Shall the minister tell the people where else he speaks, so that they will know how much he is appreciated elsewhere? Or shall he be quiet about it, so that they will have no doubt that he is earning his salary in his own parish? Be that as it may, look at this listing from the bulletin of Peoples Church of Chicago, where Dr. Preston Bradley, the city's most famed preacher, is celebrating his fiftieth anniversary as pastor:

DR. BRADLEY'S ENGAGEMENTS

Nov. 24—Worked in Study.

Nov. 25—Funeral.

Nov. 26—Sermon, Peoples Church. Sermon, National Convention, Showmen's League of America. Chicago Sunday Evening Forum with Mr. Dugald Semple of Fairlie, Scotland. Made recording at Rev. Virgil A. Kraft's.

Nov. 27—Worked in Study. Sick calls.

Nov. 28—Address, Esther Clamage Auxiliary, Windermere Hotel. Conference luncheon.

Nov. 29—Conference luncheon. Banquet for Father Gallagher.

Nov. 30—Luncheon given by Ward Quaal, Exec. V.P. and Gen. Mgr. WGN, Inc. Cut five 15-minute programs, WCFL. Meeting Adult Education Council —Roger Stevens of N.Y.

A friend of ours from Iowa saw that list and volunteered to try out the scheme with *his* activities:

Dec. 12—Overhauled auto at 103,000-mile mark. Cleaned two chickens for Bazaar.

Dec. 13—Address at F.F.A., "Organic or Inorganic Fertilizer and the Christian Church." Took children to basketball game.

Dec. 14—Delivered posters advertising Christmas concert. Refereed between women fighting about their places in Bazaar program's "acknowledgments" list.

Dec. 15—Appeared in court: forgot to write "Rev." on driver's license.

Dec. 16—Bought bus ticket for freedom ride. Bus snowed in. Repaired flat tire.

Dec. 17—Helped thaw frozen plumbing in church. Transported children for Christmas pageant practice. Painted two angels, sanded and varnished crib. Dickered with auto dealer; overhaul did not work.

Dec. 18—Work in study, 3 A.M. to 4 A.M. Preached in own church. Caught cold; missed pageant.

Dec. 19—Read *Tropic of Cancer;* found it fits inside dust jacket of a John Barclay Biblical Commentary. Dropped book out of dust jacket while at dentist's. Met with Vestry to explain situation.

Dec. 20—Spoke to church federation on "My Inward Theological Growth."

And you think one cannot learn about the Busy Church from Sunday bulletins?

The End of
a Crusade

This week we conclude our three-week crusade to bring about some changes in those ubiquitous journalistic enterprises known as Sunday church bulletins. Along the way we observed that the bulletins, designed to point to the day's hymns and masses, weekly meetings and suppers, are increasingly being given over to moralizing. We tried to de-moralize them. Now we undertake to improve on the material in those books which suggest "fillers" for Sunday bulletins—most of which we have found uninteresting. Try out these little items, ye parsons and lay editors, to enliven your parish papers:

"I'm a girl who just can't go to sleep immediately. I lie there and think about life in general."—*Tuesday Weld.*

The ten volumes of Arnold Toynbee's *A Study of History* are being reprinted in Oxford paperbacks. They contain nineteen thousand footnotes.

"Fritz would have been a great violinist if he had only practiced."—*Mrs. Fritz Kreisler.*

"Morality is very Square these days."—*Mort Sahl.*

A company in New Jersey now offers Personalized Tea Bags. You can raise funds fast, gain continuous monthly income for your group, and help the Christian Mighty Army March Forth as to War thereby. Each box and each tea bag label is individually printed with your group's name; e.g., "The 1984 Society."

"Days" to observe on the church calendar: February 21—Anniversary of the Dedication of the Washington Monument. March 3—Anniversary of the Child Labor Law. March 7—Masaryk Day. March 26—Anniversary of the Milwaukee Public School Music Festival. Let us all remember these days in our intercessions; liturgical material will be provided.

If you find a mistake in this paper, please consider that it was put there on purpose. We publish something for everyone, including those who are always looking for mistakes. [We must confess that we borrowed that one intact from the editors of the church bulletin of the First Congregational Church in San Diego, California. Cowards!]

Spike heels on the shoes of women who rode the Staten Island ferry last year cost New York City's Department of Marine and Aviation $2,313.80 for emergency inspection and repairs.

"I'd like to go back to teaching. As a matter of fact, I'd like to drop out of sight altogether."—*Charles Van Doren.*

Forward. Onward. Upward. Outward. Downward.

The End

10 Penultimate Concerns

What Is Pen-ultimate?

Saints like Simeon Stylites don't just grow on pillars, you know. So when the Simeon who stood atop this column was sainted, the page passed into the hands of sinners. We decided to use it to chronicle the fabulous but not foibleless part the religious enterprise plays in the culture of the 1960s. Growing response tells us the venture is catching on. Many readers send us items which we freely plagiarize. But others sometimes miss our intent, so perhaps we should try to introduce ourselves.

"Pen-ultimate," appearing on the penultimate page of the magazine, has theological overtones: it recalls the "penultimate" matters, the "things before the last." They are to be taken very, very seriously, but not too seriously. Spinoza speaks of ultimates, the "last things": "I have made a ceaseless effort not to ridicule, nor to bewail, nor to scorn human actions, but to understand them." But the path of such humaneness and humanity is cluttered with the debris of penultimates, and this must be cleared away with no gentle hand. Here is where columns are born—but also where misunderstandings arise.

For instance, we recently pointed a disrespectful finger at certain pseudo religious attitudes by parodying them in the form of prayers addressed to "He," "The Man Upstairs," "Someone in the Great Somewhere." To our surprise, some of our readers rose up in holy wrath; they thought we were talking about God. But we were only sweeping off the shelf some homemade household or jukebox gods that stand in the way of the Ultimate.

Another instance: A few weeks ago one of the editors wandered into a large, very well-appointed religious bookstore. He wanted to buy the theology book most debated by Methodists this year. Its author is Methodist; his face stared from the cover of the then current Methodist preachers' journal. The bookstore was Methodist. But not only was the book not known, the author was not known either—and the information clerk did not know where the theology section was. We thought such a gap should be taken very, very seriously but not too seriously. In other words, we thought it was funny in a quiet way. So did a number of readers, including some Methodists.

We were speaking in parables; it just happened that the incident happened where we said it did. You could insert "Baptist" or "Lutheran" or "Episcopalian" and the pattern of missed communication between theology and marketing would still hold. We hoped our readers understood this. But from the store's management we received a disturbed letter. The letter told us that one saleslady well recalled the incident: two brash, "erudite" young men barging into the store and lampooning certain of the items for sale. Whoever those men were, they were not from the *Century;* the real incident involved but one shy, browsing editor whom the rest of us have yet to catch raising his voice.

Is a religious bookstore too solemn an enterprise to stand a little ribbing? We hope not. Pen-ultimate is no "Candid Camera"; it does not "pick on" the nameless, faceless people who seek privacy and obscurity. We poke around among our peers in the open world of communications, events, advertising, merchandising, publicity, display. What we see often seems amusing when we look through telescopes or microscopes—or into mirrors. Saints? No. But sinners, we are told, also have their place, pen-ultimately, in the Kingdom.

Simeon's Spirit
Pays a Visit

PEN-ULTIMATE (*looking up from desk, bewildered*): Can it be? Are you the spirit of Christmas past?

SIMEON STYLITES (*who has entered quietly and taken the stance of a kibitzer*): Don't you recognize me? I used to write this column; now I haunt it. I came by to talk about the spirit of Christmas future.

P. U. (*still at desk, bewitched*): I'm having enough trouble putting together a column on the spirit of Christmas present.

S. S.: What do you mean?

P. U. (*rising and beginning to pace*): Well, you had it easy in the old days; you wrote columns of fiction and fancy. It was easy to talk about Christmas then. These days we deal with fact. And there's not much to say about Christmas this year.

S. S.: That's what I can't understand about this younger generation. I wish you would stop trying to demythologize my world. Do you think St. John's-by-the-Gas-Station and all my other sites were unreal? Often there was true "peace on earth" in *my* world. I'm a bit less happy about the world of fact you talk about every week.

P. U. (*humbled but unwilling to capitulate*): What do you make of today's facts?

S. S.: *Facts?* I have a hard time believing that what you talk about are facts. Testing fifty-megaton bombs! And do you mean to say it isn't *fantastic* to talk about neutron bombs which will destroy only man, not machines and skyscrapers? And then this business—how un-Christmasy it sounds—about fallout shelters. I can see it now: "There was no room for him in the shelter." And all these Christian crusades against next-door neighbors—they're *fact*? I thought you just dreamed them up to compete with what you call my fantasies.

P. U.: I don't think I'll even try to explain all that's been happening in the year since you were translated to your

Higher Pillar. You Simeons who run around within the guardrails on top of your pillars don't know what real life is like.

S. S.: You've got me all wrong. Simeon No. 1, the guy who died 'way back in 459, did climb away from things. But I involved myself; my pillar kept getting lower and lower. I really enjoyed the life around me. So you don't like my pillar? Well, I don't like the name of your column.

P. U.: Too eggheadish? Well, you can have your column back any time you want—or how about a Simeon No. 3?

S. S.: I reincarnate only about every fifteen hundred years.

P. U.: Well then, you'll just have to put up with our world of fact. And besides, we don't take things too seriously. Our column deals with "the things before the last." We are trying to say that such things are very, very important, but not too important.

S. S.: I think neutron bombs are *too* important.

P. U.: I liked you better when you dealt with fancy.

S. S.: For the last time, can't you get this straight? The line you are taking doesn't help anyone. Take Christmas, for example: You are having trouble because you are too earthbound; you *need* a pillar—at least a short one—so that once in a while you can climb up and listen to some of the "Glorias." You ought to hear them from where I sit up there. And *that's* fact.

P. U.: Couldn't you have your friends sing a little louder? It would help us a lot if they could be heard down here, in the middle of things. And it would be nice if you'd beam a little of your love-kindling music to Moscow; to Belmont, Massachusetts; to the Senate Office Building in Washington; to the governor's mansion in Little Rock . . .

S. S.: And to 407 South Dearborn, Chicago?

P. U.: *Alleluia!*

S. S.: That's it! That's the note I've been after all year!

817
M   JUN 30 83   MP 46753

Marty, Martin E
Pen-ultimates.

SEP   4   1 2 0 0 6

817   Marty, Martin E
M   Pen-ultimates.

Wilmington Public Library
Wilmington, N. C.

―――――

RULES

1. Books marked 7 days may be kept one
week. Books marked 14 days, two weeks. The
latter may be renewed, if more than 6 months old.

2. A fine of two cents a day will be charged
on each book which is not returned according to
above rule.   No book will be issued to any person having a fine of 25 cents or over.

3. A charge of ten cents will be made for
mutilated plastic jackets.   All injuries to books
beyond reasonable wear and all losses shall be
made good to the satisfaction of the Librarian.

4. Each borrower is held responsible for all
books drawn on his card and for all fines accru-
ing on the same.